EASY WOOD CARVING FOR CHILDREN

Disclaimer - please read carefully

Many of the activities in this book require the use of a whittling knife and/or other wood working tools. These tools should not be handled by children under the age of seven and, after that age, only under supervision from a responsible adult. Safety tips can be found on p. 11 of this book; however, please follow common sense on the handling of sharp tools. The Publisher accepts no liability for damages and injury of any kind.

Knives are tools, not toys, and should never be brought to school or into a social situation but only carried when you have a reason to do so. Please familiarise yourself with local laws on carrying knives in your country or state.

Translated by Anna Cardwell
Photographs: Per Rasmussen and Lillian Egholm
Illustrations and diagrams: Lillian Egholm
First published in German as
Das große Buch vom Schnitzen
by Verlag Freies Geistesleben, Stuttgart in 2015
This English edition published by Floris Books,
Edinburgh in 2018
Ninth printing 2023

British Library CIP Data available
ISBN 978-178250-515-0
Printed in China through
Asia Pacific Offset Ltd

Printed on sustainably sourced FSC® certified paper. Uses plant-based inks which reduce chemical emissions.

Acknowledgements

A big thank you to the children of the Rudolf Steiner School in Vordingborg for many years of inspiring lessons whittling together.

A huge thank you to my wife Lillian Egholm for her help with the text, photos, decorations, the beautiful sketches and particularly for the inspiration leading to my whittling ideas.

To finish, a thank you to the imaginative and inventive whittling artists Hussain Skotte and Balder Egholm, my son.

EASY WOOD CARVING FOR CHILDREN

Fun Whittling Projects for Adventurous Kids

Frank Egholm

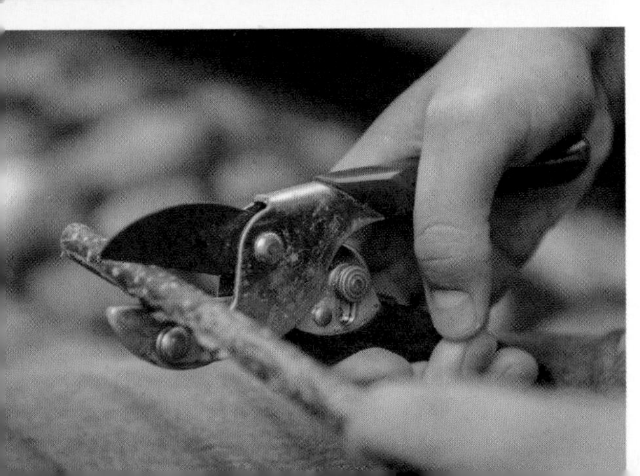

CONTENTS

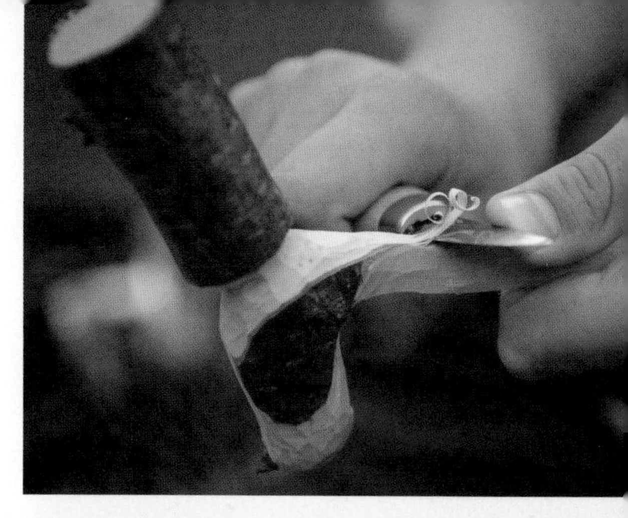

Animal figures

Games

Toys

Toys (continued)

Jewellery

Home and garden

INTRODUCTION

Wood carving, or whittling, is a fun and relaxing pastime that promotes a peaceful and creative atmosphere. This book hopes to encourage children who are new to the activity, as well as providing inspiration for experienced whittlers.

Whittling is an inherent part of our culture. In the past, predominantly boys and men carved useful items like spoons and knives for the kitchen or toys for children, and in rural areas it wasn't uncommon for most boys to be able to whittle a willow flute without any problem.

Today, wood carving is an inclusive and rewarding hobby for everyone: girls, boys, old and young. Not only does it promote concentration and creativity, it also has lots of practical advantages:

- You only need a few tools
- It is easy to make a range of decorative and useful objects
- You can find all the materials in nature, making wood carving a "green hobby"

Difficulty levels

Children can start learning to whittle between the ages of six and eight, although it depends on the development of each individual child. The activities featured in this book aim to give children a basic understanding of how to use a knife as a tool and demonstrate the possibilities wood offers as a working material.

To encourage and challenge both new and experienced wood carvers, this book contains projects of varying difficulty, indicated at the beginning of each new activity by a star rating, ranging from simple to challenging:

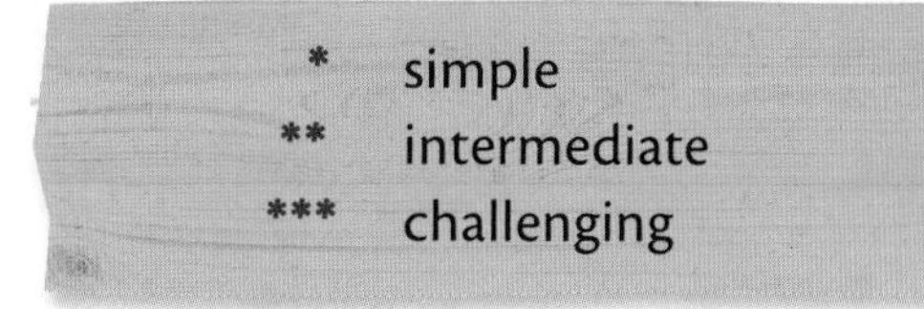

Note that projects graded with * or ** stars can be refined to make them more difficult for whittlers who are more advanced.

The sizes of the projects given are approximate values. You should decide for yourself how big you would like your finished project to be.

Whittling guidelines

1. A responsible adult should always be present.
2. Always sit when wood carving (unless instructed otherwise).
3. Make sure you are an adequate distance from other carvers.
4. Whittle away from your body (unless you have already learnt other techniques) and take care not to whittle too close to your legs.
5. Keep the knife close to the work and put it back in its sheath when not in use.
6. Don't poke into the wood with the tip of the knife.
7. If necessary, wear a glove to protect the hand holding the work.
8. A sharp knife is dangerous; a blunt knife can be even more so. Make sure your knives are always in a good condition.
9. Store knives out of the reach of children. Knives can be kept in a knife block when not in use.
10. Always keep a complete first aid kit nearby in case of emergencies.
11. Please use your own judgement as to whether safety glasses and goggles should be worn when working with wood.

GETTING STARTED

Finding a whittling knife

A knife with a blade 6–7 cm (2½ in) long is suitable for most projects in this book, but children can also use slightly larger or smaller knives, depending on what feels comfortable and manageable. Knives with a fixed blade are preferable: pocket knives with a folding blade can be dangerous as the blade can suddenly snap shut or even break off. Very young children just learning to whittle should start with a potato peeler and practise by stripping bark off a branch.

When they are ready, they should then progress to a knife with a blunt tip, as it is much safer. You can purchase a blunt tip knife, or simply sand the tip of a normal wood carving knife (knife 2 on the photo below) or even stick a strong length of sticky tape around the blade (knives 3 and 4). If you require a knife with more protection, there are lots on the market that come equipped with a cross-guard (see photo on p. 22). Finding the right knife can seem daunting, but there are lots of good knives available for a range of budgets, and individual knives and whittling sets are now widely available both on the internet and in specialist craft shops.

Protective gear

A responsible adult should decide whether a child needs to wear a glove on the hand holding the whittling project. Normal child-sized work gloves give a certain amount of protection, but you can also get cut-resistant gloves made out of Kevlar and other specialist materials. Single fingers (thumb and forefinger) can be protected with leather thumb or finger guards. Remember, a glove can never give complete protection: children should always work carefully and never use the tip of the knife as a stabbing tool.

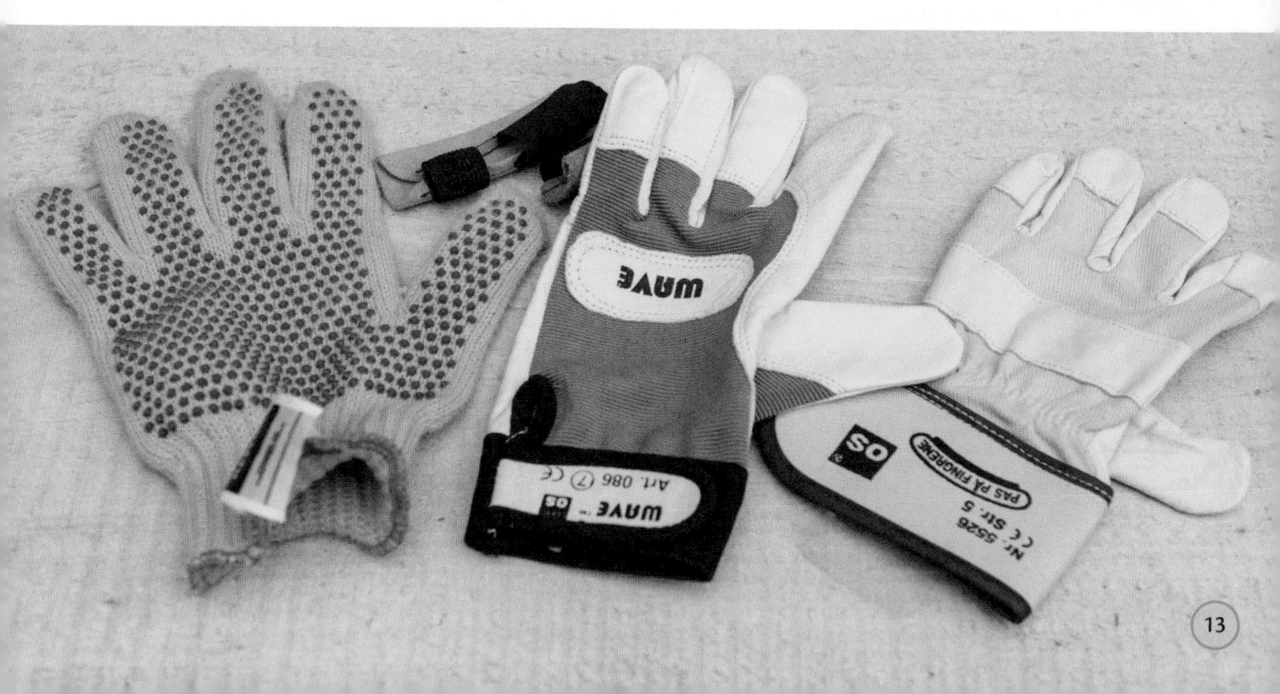

Wood

Most projects in this book are suited to fresh branches. They are generally easier to work with than dry wood, and material from deciduous trees such as hazel, birch, alder, poplar, willow and lime wood (basswood) give the best results.

Branches and trunks of fast-growing trees provide the perfect working material, as knotty or slow-growing wood can be a challenge to carve. The shape of a tree's branches gives rise to many possibilities, so it's always worth considering whether a particular wood will suit how you want your final project to look. For instance, you should always choose bark that is thin and hard (e.g. hazel) for whittling intricate patterns. Hazel usually has dark bark that contrasts beautifully with its light wood when carved.

Making a larger project takes time. If you need to take a break but want to work on a project again later, keep the wood in a cool place and, if possible, wrap it in plastic. However, be careful as wrapped wood can mould, especially light wood such as alder and willow. You can also keep fresh sticks in the freezer for use at a later point, but make sure to remove them before they show signs of rotting. You should ideally leave whittling wood to dry outdoors, but you can dry finished projects in a cool place such as a garage, workshop or shed. Although it can seem like a test of patience waiting for a project to dry (especially for excited children), make sure to take extra care with larger pieces as they can crack if dried too quickly.

Where to find fresh branches

Anyone who has access to a garden or nearby woodland should have an adequate supply of fresh branches, but it's important to ask permission first if the land is not your own. Most gardeners, tree surgeons and landowners are happy to give away suitable whittling sticks when they trim or cut down bushes, and people are often delighted to have their garden trees trimmed for free and the wood disposed of usefully. If you do have permission to take branches, it can be helpful to carry a small folding saw when out on a walk; the perfect branch may just turn up unexpectedly.

After Christmas it should be easy to find suitable whittling wood thanks to discarded Christmas trees: the projects on pages 127 and 129 are all made out of the tip of discarded Christmas trees.

Dry wood

For some of the projects in this book dry wood is more suitable than fresh branches. A square block of lime wood (basswood) is particularly good for beginners as it is still very soft when dry and will be easy to work with. Lime wood can be found at some garden centres, wood stores and craft stores, as well as specialist wood suppliers online. Alternatively, if you find felled poplars you can gather a larger amount of wood and use it later. A square block of wood is hard to hold and its shape gives less scope for variations, but you are not dependent on finding fresh branches and can work on your project over a longer period of time.

Dry wood and fresh branches often have knots or a twisted growth that make it difficult to carve, especially for children, so take care, but feel free to use dry branches for small, simple projects.

WOOD CARVING TECHNIQUES

Wood carving requires concentration and care. Be particularly attentive when learning a new wood carving technique; making sure you are whittling correctly from the start reduces the risk of accidents and encourages good technique.

Whittling away from the body

1. The basic technique

- Hold the wood with one hand and the knife with the other.
- Make sweeping cuts away from you along the grain of the wood – this is a good technique for long cuts. You won't always have the knife completely under control when using this technique, so take care.
- Whilst sitting, splay your legs or bend them to one side so you don't cut into them.
- Lead the knife slightly sideways; this gives you the best cutting technique.

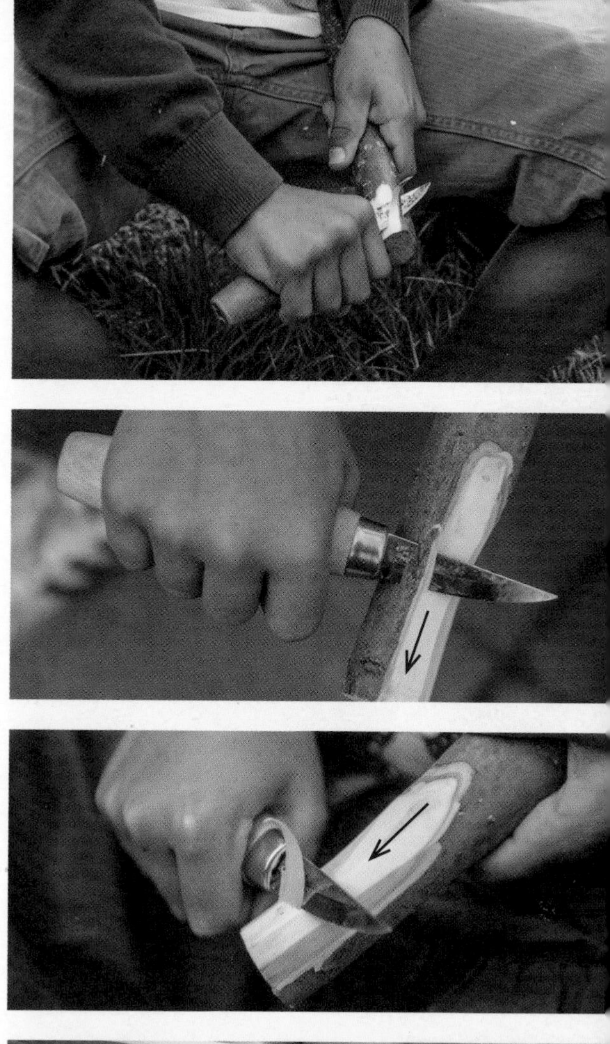

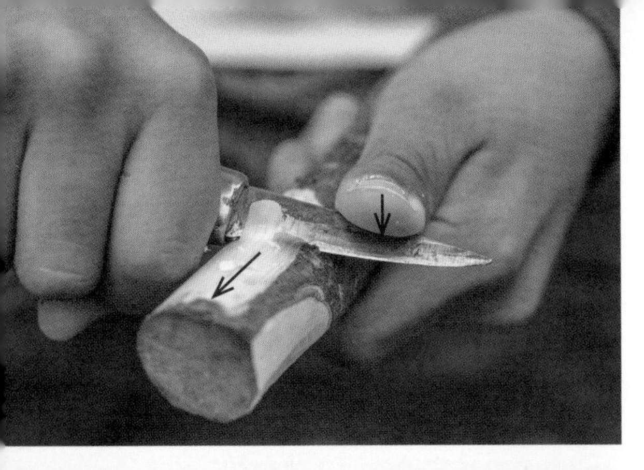

2. The thumb push technique

This technique is suitable for detailed and controlled wood carving.

- Press the thumb of the hand holding the wood against the blunt side of the blade to push and guide the knife forwards.
- At the same time, move the knife slightly up and down. Your thumb may get sore to start with, so stick a plaster over it first!
- This technique is used for cutting into wood or if you need to make a groove. Don't forget to turn the work when necessary so you're always whittling *away* from your body.

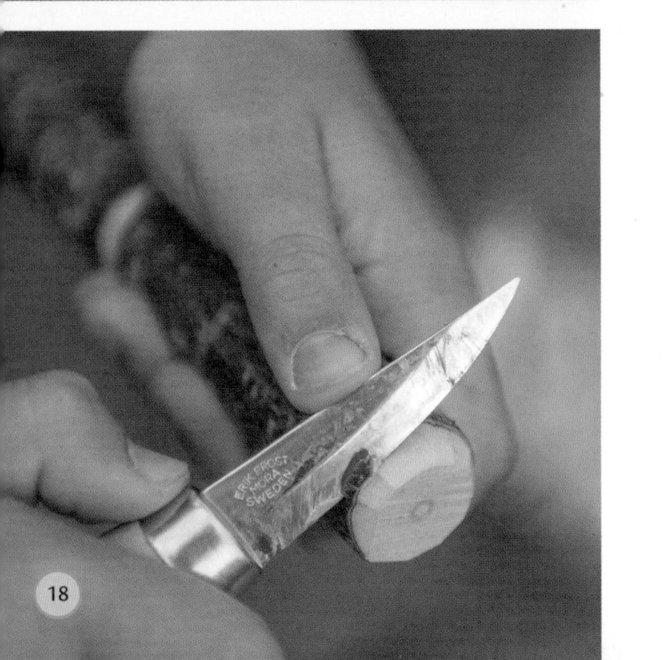

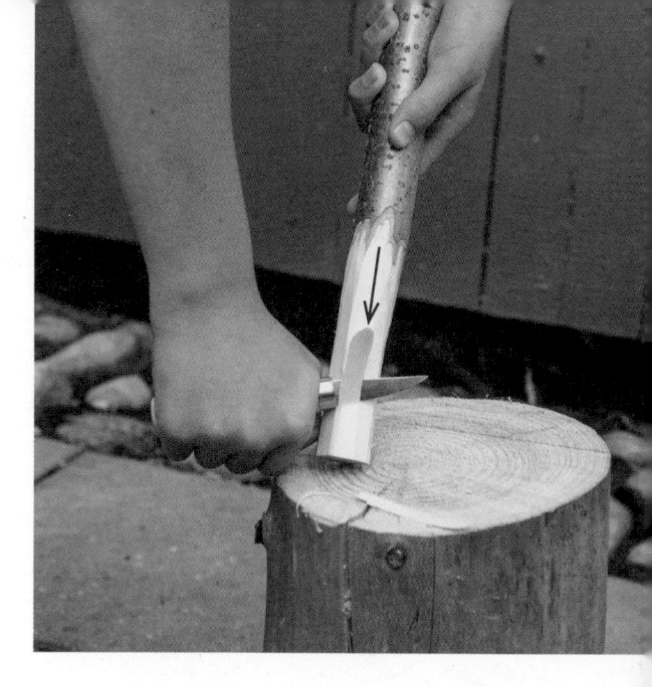

3. The scissor technique

This technique (see photo above) is well suited to rough cuts.

- Hold your hands close to your body.
- Push the knife forward while pulling the wood back.

Tip: You can also use this method of holding both the knife and the wood for the thumb push technique (opposite).

4. Whittling against wood

For this technique you'll have to whittle standing up, which is the exception to the "sitting down" guideline detailed earlier.

- Push the knife against the wood piece and whittle *down*.
- The advantage of this method is that you can use more pressure. This is especially useful when whittling long cuts, for example if you want to remove bark from a branch.

Whittling towards the body

If necessary, wear a protective glove when using the following techniques.

5. Working an end piece (the pull stroke)

This technique is a good supplement to the thumb push technique (p. 18) if you are working on an end piece.

- Hold the knife as shown in the top photo (left).
- Move it up and down slightly while keeping your thumb pressed securely against the work piece from the other side.

6. The thumb support

- Let the thumb of the hand holding the knife rest against the wood piece to provide some stability.
- Whittle by guiding the knife in small circular movements with your other fingers or carefully pushing it forwards.
- It is very important that your thumb keeps the work piece stable – if not, the knife could slip and cut into the hand holding the wood.

Tip: Practise this technique without wood – hold the knife between your fingers and move it up and down without touching your thumb.

7. The double thumb technique

- Hold the knife as described in the previous technique using the additional thumb support.
- Press the thumb of the other hand holding the wood against the blunt side of the blade. This gives excellent control over small cuts performed towards your body.
- Either whittle with small rotating movements or push the knife into the wood using even pressure.
- Always be careful! The knife hand should only make small, careful movements.

8. Using a whittling board

You can make a whittling board out of a simple piece of plywood. Drill holes at one end for a length of string so that it can be worn around the neck, and cover it with a piece of fabric or leather so the surface is not too smooth and slippery.

- Press the end of the wood against your chest using the board as protection.
- Carve towards your body with careful movements, the knife should not touch the board.
- Use a different but appropriate technique for whittling the part of the wood that is actually touching the board.

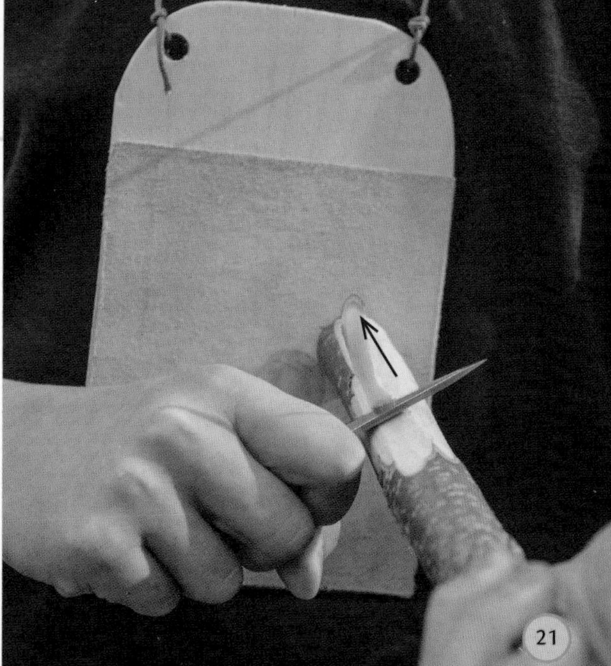

PRACTICAL TIPS

Sharpening knives

There are different types of sharpening stones with both coarse and fine grain size. If your knife is very blunt, you will need to use a coarser stone, followed by a finer one. Water, petroleum or honing oil can be used for lubricating wet sharpening stones, but diamond and ceramic sharpening stones can be used dry.

How to sharpen your knife

- Place the knife on the stone at an angle, usually 20–25°.
- Move the knife across the stone in circular movements or back and forth.

Tip: An electric wet sharpening machine is useful particularly if you have a lot of knives to sharpen.

Saws and garden shears

You can use a normal saw for cutting blocks of wood and garden shears for very thin branches, but a folding pruning saw is most effective for regular branches. It is not a suitable tool for children and must only ever be used by a responsible adult. Jigsaws, band saws and fret saws are best for fine, intricate work.

Splitting wood

It's easy to split wood lengthwise. If possible, split it in the centre (see Figure 1). You can then split each half, or the thicker half, into quarters (as shown in Figure 2).

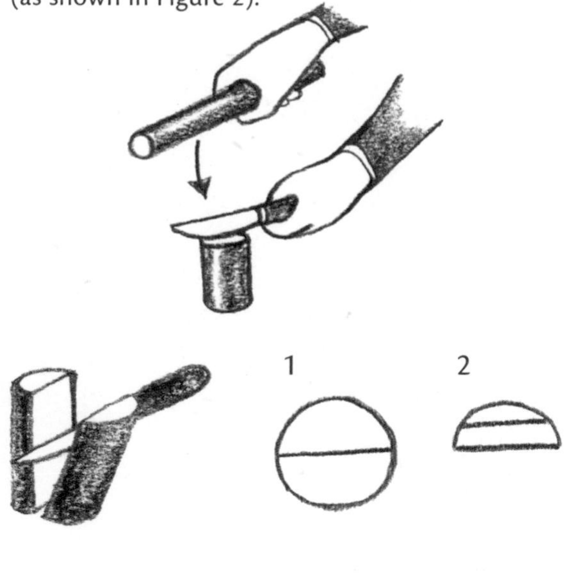

Colouring wood

As you will see, some wood carving projects require paint or oil to achieve a finished look. In these cases, the wood needs to be completely dry before you colour it. You can use acrylic paint as it dries quickly, but keep in mind that a thick layer can hide the natural quality of the wood. Water-based oil paints can also be used, but again, only use a thin layer as the paint dries slowly and can crack. Wood stains, like water based colours, give a sheer covering and are good for large areas but not for fine detail. Children can also use wax crayons or coloured pencils to decorate their projects. If you would prefer to not to colour your project, oil (for example, raw linseed oil) is good for impregnating the surface and providing both shine and protection.

Sanding wood

The surface of sanded wood is smooth and fine, and the process can be a satisfying, soothing experience. A number of projects in this book are particularly suited to sanding, for example the small rattles on p. 99.

It is important to finish whittling before you sand. If you whittle after sanding, the grains of the sanding paper embedded in the wood will blunt your knife. The surface of the wood also needs to be completely dry.

It is best to sand with a rough sandpaper (80–100 grit) first and then finish with finer paper (120–180 grit).

Carving seat

If you're an experienced whittler, you can build a carving seat – a seat with an arm – for younger children to sit in a good whittling position (see photos). A small ridge at the front holds the workpiece in place and makes the whittling process a little easier.

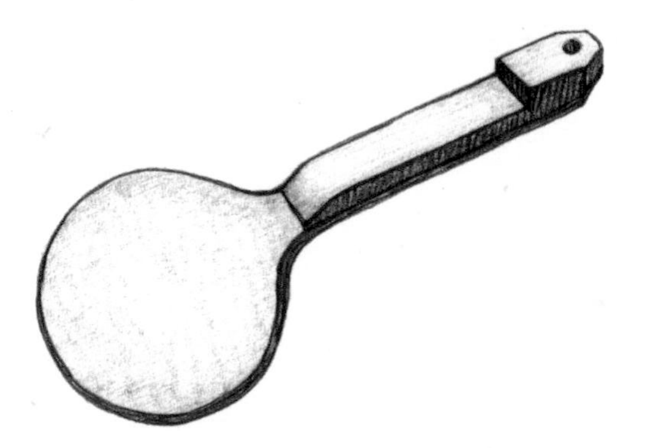

Whittling and reading

Sitting with friends making something beautiful out of a piece of wood can be very satisfying, but whittling is also a great opportunity to chat and tell stories.

This fairy tale, written by Hans Christian Andersen (1805–1875) is well suited to wood carving. This version of the tale is easily accessible online but it can be good to sometimes substitute words or phrases to suit your audience.

Luck may lie in a button

I'll tell you a story about luck. Some know good luck day in, day out; others only now and then in their lucky seasons; and there are some people who know it only once in a lifetime. But luck comes at some time or other to us all.

Now I need not tell you what everyone knows, that it is God who puts little children in their mother's lap. What you may not know, is that when God leaves the child he always leaves it a lucky object. He doesn't put it where the child is born, but tucks it away in some odd corner of the earth where we least expect it.

This lucky object may turn out to be an apple. That was the case with one man called Newton. The apple fell into his lap, and his luck came with it. But I've a different story to tell, about a pear.

Once there was a man born poor, who married without a penny. He was a turner by trade, but as he made nothing except umbrella handles and umbrella rings, he didn't earn much money.

"I'll never find my luck," he would say.

Wild berries grew around the man's house and garden as if they were the richest ornament. However, in the garden was also a pear tree. It had never borne fruit; yet the man's luck lay hidden in the tree.

One night the wind blew in a terrible gale, and a large branch was torn from the pear tree. It was brought into the workshop and, as a joke, the turner made from it wooden pears of all sizes.

"For once, my tree has borne pears," he smiled, and gave them to his children for playthings.

The turner's family had only one umbrella between them, and when the wind blew hard, their umbrella would blow inside out. Sometimes it would break, and the button and loop that held it closed would always fly off just as they thought they had the umbrella neatly folded.

One day it popped off, and the turner hunted for it everywhere. In a crack of the floor he came across one of the smallest pears he had given to his children as a toy.

"If I can't find the button," he said, "I'll make this do." He fitted a string through it, and the little pear buttoned up the umbrella perfectly. It was the best umbrella fastener ever.

The next time the turner sent umbrella handles and umbrella rings to the city, he added several of the small wooden pears. They were fitted to a few new umbrellas, and put with a thousand others on a ship bound for America. The Americans saw that the little pears held better than the other umbrella buttons, and the merchant gave orders that from now on all the umbrellas should be fastened with little wooden pears.

That was a lot of work! Thousands of pears had to be made for all the umbrellas that went to America. The turner used up the whole pear tree. The pears earned pennies that grew into a lot of money.

"My luck was in that pear tree all along," the man said. Soon he had a great factory with plenty of workers to help him. Now that he always had time for jokes he would say, "Good luck may lie in a button."

ANIMAL FIGURES

BIRD MADE FROM A SINGLE BRANCH*

You will need

- Branch wood, diameter 2.5 cm (1 in), length 12 cm (5 in)
- Slice of branch, diameter 3 cm (1 ¼ in) and 2–3 cm (1 in) thick to make a stand
- Dowel, diameter 5–6 mm (¼ in)
- Whittling knife
- Drill with a bit the same size as the dowel, 5–6 mm (13/64 in)
- Ink, coloured pencils or paint for decoration

How to make it

1. Shape the bird's beak and body by whittling away the wood above the head and below the body. Narrow the tail slightly.
2. Leave the bark in the shape of the wings.
3. Drill a hole in the stand and in the underside of the bird. As illustrated in the figures, the angle of the hole determines whether the bird will look up or down.
4. Position the bird by pushing the dowel into the drilled holes in the bird and the stand.
5. Draw eyes and a beak with ink, coloured pencils or paint.

Note: You can also use this bird for the seesaw toy on p. 86.

BIRD WITH A FEATHERY TAIL**

You will need

- Y–shaped branch, (as shown in the figure), diameter 2.5–3.5 cm (1–1 ½ in). Make sure the tail part of the forked branch is long enough to hold while whittling the tail feathers.
- Whittling knife
- Hand saw or folding pruning saw
- Ink, coloured pencils or paint for decoration (optional)

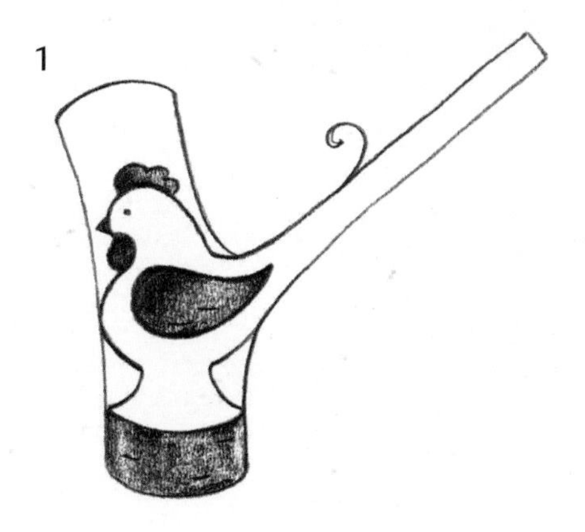

For this project you can either whittle a rooster or a bird with a simpler head. The focus of this particular task is the tail, although you can choose whether you want to leave bark for some wings too.

How to make it

1. Saw the branch to the length you want it, making sure you can hold the figure while you whittle.
2. Carve the head first, then the body by cutting into the branch.
3. Narrow the tail at the sides, but leave the top so you still have enough wood to make the bird's feathery tail.
4. For good curling, let the branch dry for one or two days before carving the tail feathers.
5. Make the tail feathers by holding the tail piece and pushing the knife forwards along the grain with your thumb (see Figure 1).
6. Trim the shape of the tail and any excess wood.
7. Decorate the bird with ink or paint if you want to.

Note: This feathering or shaving technique for the bird's tail is also used for the straw flower project on p. 109.

BIRD MADE FROM THE END OF A BRANCH**

You will need

- Branch wood, diameter 2.5–3 cm (1–1 ¼ in)
- Whittling knife
- Sandpaper (for a smooth finish)
- Ink or paint for decoration (optional)

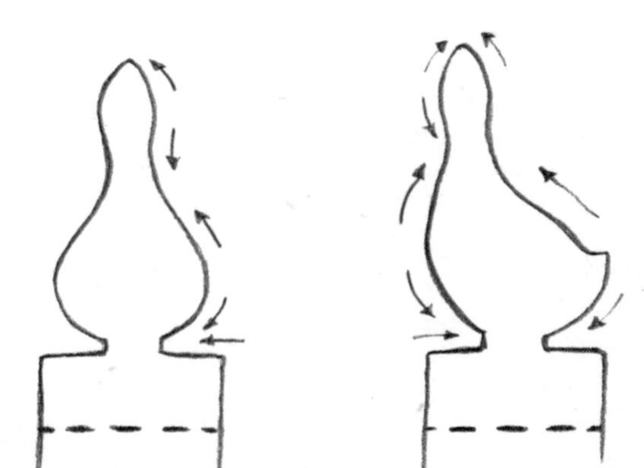

This project uses the end of a branch to form the bird's base and shape. Practise whittling towards your body before attempting this slightly more difficult piece.

You can carve your bird into whichever position you prefer, or if you have time, perhaps practise by making a variety of birds. As examples, the bird on the far right of the photo opposite is a simple shape sitting on a nest. The central bird's body is well formed with a carved lower body, while the white hen's tail is whittled out of a small side twig. The goose (far left) has been sanded down to give a smooth finish, which is always an alternative to the rougher whittled surface.

How to make it

1. Using the figures for reference, whittle in the direction of the arrows to give the bird its shape.
2. To give your bird a smooth finish, rub with sandpaper until the surface is even all over.
3. If you want to, decorate the bird with ink or paint.

LIFELIKE BIRD***

You will need

- Dry lime wood (basswood), 3–5 cm (1 ¼–2 in) thick
- Branch for use as a stand or foot
- Whittling knife
- Fret saw, band saw or jigsaw
- Drill
- Wood glue
- Screws
- Metal wire,1.5–2 mm (1⁄16 in)
- Small black beads for the eyes
- Ink or paint for decoration

You will need plenty of time for this project, and it may be helpful to print out a photo of the kind of bird you would like to make for your reference while you whittle and paint. Dry lime wood (basswood) is best for a project of this kind, but you can position the bird on any surface you like, for example a Y-shaped branch or a piece of split wood.

Tip: To make a lifelike bird you will need to carefully consider the shape: where does the neck begin and how thick is it? Is the body thin or round? What shape is the beak? Is the head round or narrow? Make sure the tail isn't too short or too pointed, and try not to remove too much wood around the head or beak.

How to make it

1. Copy a bird from a picture in the size you would like your project to be; this is quite simple if you trace the outlines using tracing paper and make a template for carving on the wood (see photo on previous page). Make sure the outlines follow the wood's grain so the beak or tail does not split off later.
2. If you want the bird's beak to point downwards, whittle the bird without a beak. You can then make a beak out of a second piece of wood and glue it into a drilled hole (see Figure 2, below).
3. Saw out the bird using a fret saw, a band saw or a jigsaw. It is easier to follow the lines if you have a fine blade for this kind of intricate work.
4. Whittle away some of the edges to give the bird some shape and make the workpiece easier to hold. Continue carving the bird, carefully following its shape (see Figure 3, below – note that the head is narrower than the body but not really separate).
5. Using the thumb push technique for most of the bird (see p. 18 for details), whittle towards your body to make the back of the head. Use the arrows on Figure 1, below, for reference.
6. Hold the bird in your hand and feel whether it is rounded enough. There shouldn't be anything angular about its shape.
7. Mark the position of the bird's eyes. Black beads can be very lifelike, but if they aren't positioned correctly they can spoil the finished look of your bird. Make sure to mark the points exactly, drill carefully and not too deep and then glue the beads in place. If you don't have black beads, it's fine to use paint or ink instead.

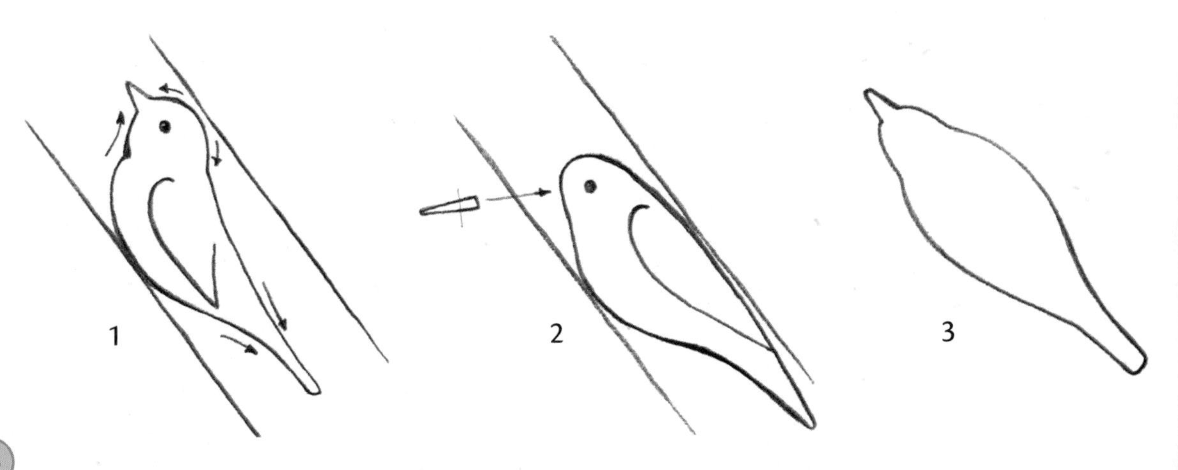

To make wire legs, drill holes in the bird and the branch. Glue the ends of the wire in place.

The bird can also sit directly on the branch (without visible legs). Drill a hole in both the underside of the bird and the branch, add glue and connect them with a short length of dowel.

Decorate with paint or ink to make your bird look as realistic as possible.

PIGS AND DOGS**

You will need

- Branch, diameter 1–3 cm (½–1¼ in), length 15 cm (6 in)
- Small whittling shavings or twigs
- Whittling knife
- Drill, same diameter as twigs
- Saw or gardening shears
- Wood glue
- Scraps of leather or fabric to decorate tails and ears
- Black paint or ink

Make these little figures as toys, decorations or for the game "Pig throwing" (see p. 49).

How to make it

1. First carve the pointed muzzle or snout, then the back of the animal.
2. Saw or cut off any excess branch length.
3. Clamp your workpiece securely, then at an angle, drill holes for the legs so they will point outwards.
4. Whittle small bits of wood or twigs as legs to fit the holes.
5. Glue the legs in place and cut them to the correct length with gardening shears.
6. Cut the leather or fabric into ear and tail shapes and secure with glue.
7. Use dots of black paint or ink for the eyes and nose.

FENCE WITH STRING OR RAILS*

You will need

- Branches, diameter 1–1.5 cm (½–¾ in)
- 2 thin dry twigs/thick wire or string
- Whittling knife
- Drill
- Saw
- Wood glue

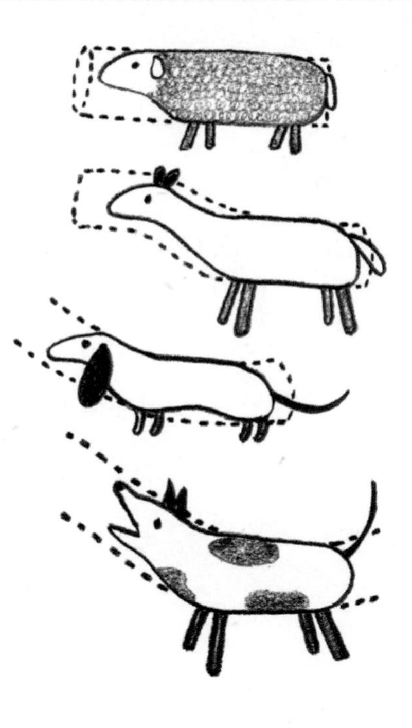

How to make it

1. Round off one end of the branches.
2. Drill two holes the same diameter as the twigs halfway through the branch.
3. Glue the twigs horizontally into the holes. If you want to make the fence with string or wire, drill two holes, diameter 2–4 mm (5/64–5/32 in bit) right through the branch and pull the string or wire through them.
4. Saw the branch to the correct length for a fence post.
5. Whittle further posts.
6. Glue the horizontal twigs in place or thread string or wire through the posts to connect the fences together.

You can also carve other animals. Some examples are shown here.

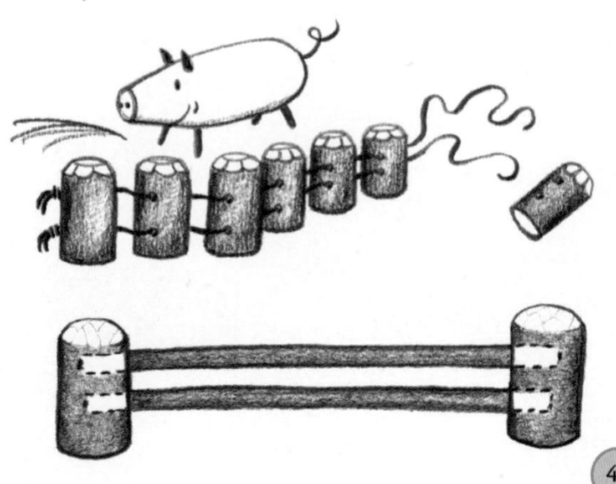

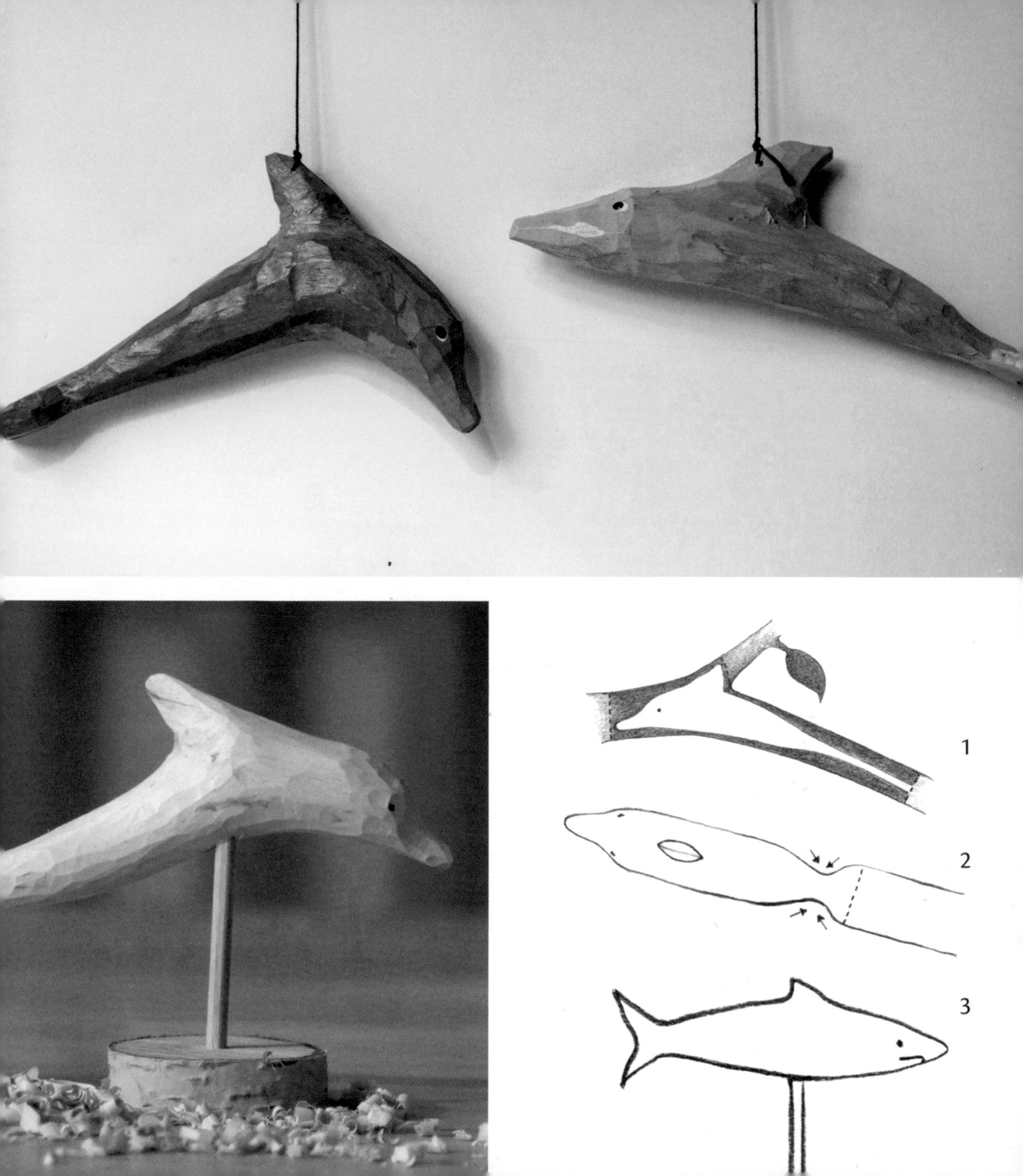
1
2
3

DOLPHIN**

You will need

- Branch with side twig, main branch 2.5 cm (1 in) diameter
- Whittling knife
- Saw
- Garden shears
- Sandpaper (if you want your dolphin to have a smooth finish)
- Black beads for the eyes
- Ink or paint for decoration (optional)

Tip: You can make different-sized dolphins and modify them for other projects:

- For hanging up; drill a hole in the dorsal fin and thread wire through it
- Mount it on a tree slice for display (see instructions for the bird project on p.31)
- Attach a chain or earring hooks to use smaller dolphin figures as jewellery (see p. 97)
- Make two dolphins and create a seesaw toy (see p. 86)

These dolphins are made out of a simple branch with a side twig for the dorsal fin. You can make your dolphin look like it's jumping out of the waves by using a curved branch.

How to make it

1. As shown in Figure 1, saw the branch to the length you would like your dolphin to be, leaving sufficient length for holding the workpiece.
2. Cut the small side branch (the dorsal fin) to the correct length using the tip of your garden shears.
3. Carve the head, then the dorsal fin. Creating the shape of the fin can be tricky at first, so whittle from the sides towards the fin to make a narrow and pointed shape.
4. Whittle into the body at the connecting point (see the arrows on Figure 2), making sure the tail is still wide enough.
5. To finish your tail, trim the holding piece with garden shears (see the dotted line on Figure 2).
6. Insert black beads for the eyes, or use a dot of black paint.
7. Decorate your dolphin with ink or paint if you want to.

Tip: You can make a shark in a similar way. To do this, carve a vertical tail instead of a horizontal one, as shown in Figure 3.

SEAL**

You will need

- Branch with side twig, main branch 2.5 cm (1 in) diameter, 10–15 cm (4–6 in) in length
- Whittling knife
- Saw
- Garden shears
- Black beads for the eyes
- Ink or paint for decoration (optional)

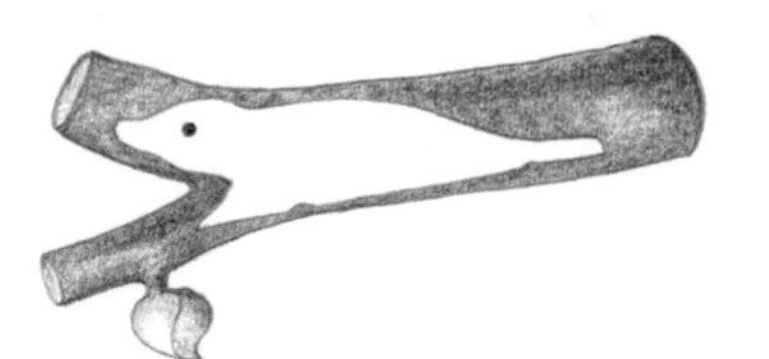

How to make it

1. Cut the branch to the correct length for your seal.
2. Carve the body, head and tail. Use the figure on this page as reference to copy the seal's shape if you need to. See the instructions on the previous page for whittling a dolphin's tail – the process is exactly the same.
3. Saw or whittle the flippers straight to give a secure standing base for the seal.
4. Insert black beads for the eyes, or use a dot of black paint.
5. If you'd like to decorate the rest of your seal, use paint or ink.

SNAKE**

You will need

- Suitably shaped branches, one end pointing up for the head and touching the ground in several places so the snake can sit securely
- Whittling knife
- Saw
- Ink or paint for decoration

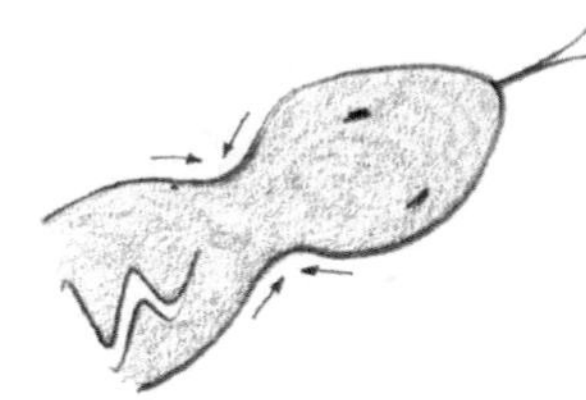

How to make it

1. Saw the branch to your preferred length.
2. Check whether the snake is lying in the correct position.
3. Carve the head and shape a narrow neck (as in the figure below), then whittle a pointed tail.
4. You can remove the bark or cut a pattern into it (hazel bark is thinner and harder and so more suited to carving patterns than willow). The corkscrew shape can make it hard to remove the bark, but in spring the bark is looser and you can simply pull it off.
5. Once the snake is dry, paint it. Don't forget to add the eyes!

GAMES

PIG THROWING*

You will need

- Branches, diameter 1–1.5 cm (½–¾ in)
- Small whittling shavings or dry twigs
- Whittling knife
- Drill, same diameter as twigs
- Saw or gardening shears
- Wood glue
- Black paint or ink

How to make it

1. You will need to make two pig figures as shown on p. 40 (steps 1–5), making sure to whittle a flat back for the pig so it can land securely on it when thrown. You won't need to add ears or a tail to the figures for your game.
2. When attaching the legs to your pig, angle them so that the pig can land either on its back legs and tail or front legs and snout.
3. Draw a spot with paint or ink on the figure's left side, otherwise you won't know which side your pig has landed on when it's thrown.

How to play (two to eight players)

Take turns to throw both pigs on a flat surface. The thrower scores points depending on which position the pigs land in. They can then choose whether to keep their points and pass their turn on to the next player, or continue playing and risk losing all their points. If the thrower doesn't get any points it's the next player's turn.

The player who reaches 100 points first wins the game.

Point system

Position	Points
Both pigs land on the same side	1
One pig lands on one side, the other on the other side *(it is the next player's turn)*	0
One pig on its back	5
Both pigs on their backs	20
One pig on its legs	5
Both pigs on their legs	20
One pig on its snout	10
Both pigs on their snouts	40
One pig on its backside	10
Both pigs on their backsides	40

1
2

GAME PIECES**

You will need

- Branches, diameter 1.5–2.5 cm (¾–1 in); length 10–15 cm (4–6 in) (for pieces with acorn cup hats, make sure the branch diameter suits the cup size)
- Scraps of leather, fabric, bark, cardboard or nutshells
- Wood glue
- Paint or coloured pencils for decoration

How to make it

1. To make a figure with a pointed hat (Figure 1) carve one end of the branch into a point.
2. Remove the bark to make the face.
3. Saw the figure to the correct length.
4. Cut out a circular piece of fabric or leather and cut a hole in the centre that matches the thickness of your branch, checking that it fits.
5. Apply glue to the branch or the inside of the brim and glue the fabric/leather ring in place.
6. Paint the top of your hat and draw on eyes and a mouth.

You can make your game pieces fun and decorative in lots of ways, for example by carving a point on one end of a sawn branch and making a hat out of leather, fabric or bark. Nutshells also make good hats, while animals with leather ears are easy to make (see Figure 2, opposite).

To play Tic Tac Toe with your figures, draw the game board on a piece of plywood, cardboard or paper. It can be any size, but should have nine equal squares (3 × 3). The rules are very simple: players alternate turns until someone gets three of their figures in a row on the board, or until all nine squares are filled.

The whittled game pieces can be used for lots of games, and you can even make new fun pieces for games you already own.

TOWER OF HANOI**

You will need

- Different-sized discs (up to seven): saw discs from dry branches so the larger discs will not split when drying
- Dowel, diameter 8 mm (approx. ½ in)
- Drill, diameter 8 and 9 mm (5⁄16 and 23⁄64 in)
- Board for the base (at least as wide and three times as long as the diameter of the largest disc)
- Wood glue
- Paint for decoration (optional)

This game is also called the "Tower of Brahma" and is a famous mathematical puzzle invented by the French mathematician, Édouard Lucas.

The game consists of three rods and a number of different-sized discs that can slide onto any rod. To start, the discs are placed in a tower in ascending order on one rod, the smallest disc on the top. The aim of the game is to stack the entire tower onto another rod to make an identical tower following only these rules:

1. You can only move one disc at a time.
2. You cannot place a larger disc on top of a smaller disc.

How to make it

1. Drill a 9 mm ($^{23}/_{64}$ in bit) hole in the centre of each disc.
2. Drill three 8 mm ($^{5}/_{16}$ in bit) holes in the base for your dowel rods; mark out their placement first and check the discs don't overlap.
3. Cut the dowels slightly longer than the complete tower and glue them in the holes.
4. If you'd like to decorate your discs you can use paint, or carve interesting shapes and patterns into the outside rim to make them even more decorative.

Background

Normally the game is played with seven discs, but you can also make a simpler version with fewer discs. With each disc that you add, the lowest number of moves required to complete the task doubles, and one extra move is added, for example one disc = one move; two discs (1 x 2 + 1) = 3 moves; three discs (3 x 2 +1) = 7 moves; four discs (7 x 2 +1) = 15 moves and so on. For seven discs you will need at least 127 moves!

This game is based on a legend. The story tells of a large temple in the centre of the world in which there is a brass platter with three diamond needles attached. When creating the world, the god Brahma placed 64 gold discs in a tower on one of the needles, the largest disc at the bottom, the others in ascending order on top of it. It is said monks were given the task of creating an identical new tower by moving the discs in accordance with the two rules above. According to the prophecy, once all 64 discs have been moved to make a new tower, the temple will turn to dust and the world will end with an enormous thunderclap.

But before you get too worried, here are some facts: with 64 discs the monks would need at least 18,446,744,073,709,551,615 moves, and even if they were fast and managed one disc per second for the entire day, it would still take them nearly 585 billion years to finish!

Background

Legend has it there was once a prince whose realm was criss-crossed with paths. Eight towers were built to overlook them, but none stood on the same path.

The prince had four map fragments of his realm that he kept in the castle treasury and he promised a large reward to anyone who could fit the pieces together correctly.

Think this task sounds easy? It's trickier than you might think – only one tower is allowed to stand on any horizontal, vertical or diagonal path.

1

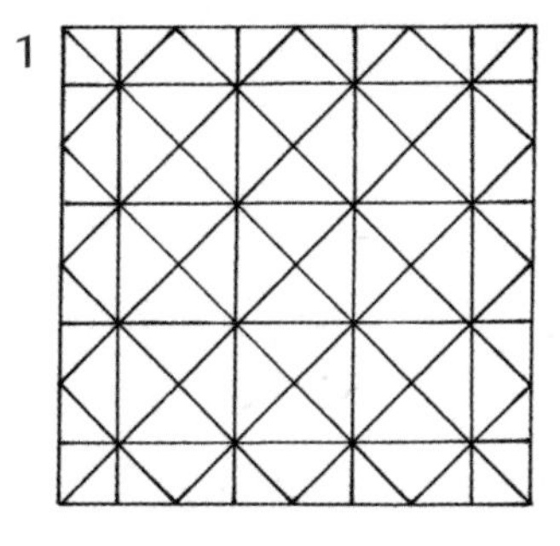

2

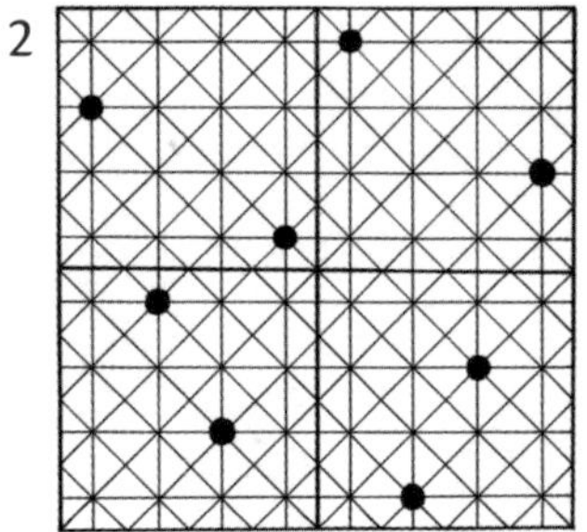

THE FOUR CONFOUNDING SQUARES*

You will need

- 4 square plywood boards, 4–6 mm (approx. ¼ in) thick, 16 x 16 cm (6 ¾ x 6 ¾ in) wide
- Branches, diameter 1–1.5 cm (½–¾ in), long enough to look like towers when screwed into your boards
- Whittling knife
- Ruler
- Drill
- 8 small screws
- Ink, permanent marker pen or paint for decoration (optional)
- Material for making extra game figures

While the boards or "fragments" for this game are simple in design, you can make the game more interesting by whittling decorated towers, for example with elaborate pinnacles or carved windows. You can also make trolls or fantasy figures to guard the paths (follow the steps for making game pieces on p. 51).

How to make it

1. Using Figure 1 as a guide, draw the illustrated grid on all four boards with ink/permanent marker and a ruler, making sure that your grid squares match up when the four boards are placed together.
2. Whittle eight towers from your branches. You can decorate them however you like, as shown in the drawing below.
3. Drill eight small holes in the boards for the towers (using the black dots in Figure 2 for placement reference) and screw the towers in place from below.
4. For the game to work, it is important that the towers are positioned correctly. The top two boards should be the same, just turned in different directions.

If you want to, you can decorate your board with paint or ink.

TOYS

1962

RACING CAR*

You will need

- Branch, diameter 4–5 cm (1½–2 in)
- Whittling knife
- 4 wood wheels (available at most craft shops or online)
- 2 dowels
- Drill, 2 mm (1/16 in) larger than the dowels
- Saw
- Wood glue
- Paint or ink for decoration (optional)

How to make it

1. Split your branch into two pieces. They should both be thick enough that they don't crack when you drill into them.
2. Whittle the front of the car, then create a more angular shape by flattening the sides. You can use a picture for reference if you need to.
3. Drill two holes through the sides of your car for the wheel shafts. They should be far enough apart that the wheels won't touch when they spin.
4. Saw the car to the right size.
5. Insert the dowels into the drilled holes and saw them down to the correct length.
6. To finish, glue the wheels to the ends of the dowels.
7. If you want to, you can now decorate your car with paint or ink.

SPINNING TOPS*

You can make lots of different kinds of spinning tops. The following pages will show you several examples: disc tops made out of branches on this page, whittled tops and tops made from an acorn. Adding a handle and a pull string will make your top spin fast!

You will need

- Branch disc, diameter 3–5 cm (1 ¼–2 in), 1–1.5 cm (½–¾ in) thick (use dry wood so your top does not split later)
- Length of dowel, diameter 5–8 mm (approx. ¼–½ in), but use 8 mm if used as a handle
- Drill, same diameter as dowel ($^{13}/_{64}$–$^{5}/_{18}$ in)
- Knife or pencil sharpener
- Wood glue (if needed)
- Sandpaper
- Paint for decoration
- Cardboard to make changeable discs (optional)

How to make it

1. Drill a hole into the centre of the branch disc; if necessary use a smaller drill first or make a small hole with an awl.
2. Make a pointed tip on the dowel with a knife or pencil sharpener.
3. Push the dowel through the hole in the disc; make sure the balance point is quite far down by positioning the disc on the lower part of the dowel. The dowel should not be too long.
4. Check whether the top spins well. If the disc doesn't sit securely on its own, glue the dowel in place.
5. You might find that the top doesn't spin properly; if so, check: is the hole in the centre of the disc? Is the hole drilled straight so the dowel is also straight? Is the disc round and cut straight? If you're having problems, it may be that the tip of the dowel is too pointed. You can flatten it a little using sandpaper.
6. Draw or paint the disc to decorate. Alternatively, draw patterns on a circle of paper and glue it to the wood. Cardboard discs are also fun to decorate and easy to change. It's always fun to see how the colours appear to "blend" when the top is spun.

SPINNING TOP WITH HANDLE AND PULL STRING**

You will need

- Spinning top with dowel, diameter 8 mm (approx. ½ in), length 8 cm (3¼ in) – see the previous page for how to make a basic spinning top
- Dry wood block (lime wood/ basswood is preferable), 2.5 x 4 x 15 cm (1 x 1½ x 6 in)
- Small thin twig for the pull string
- Drill, diameter 3.5 mm (9/64 in) and 9 mm (23/64 in)
- Whittling knife
- String or nylon thread, 50–60 cm long (20–22 in)
- Lighter/match or sticky tape

If you want your top to spin fast, give it a handle and pull string. Seeing whose top spins the longest is always an exciting game!

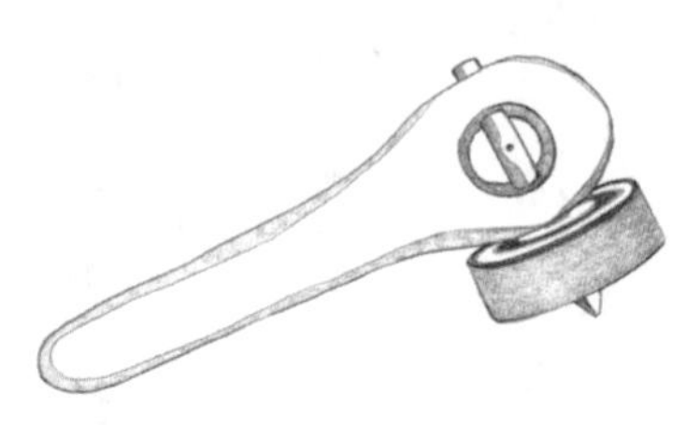

How to make it

1. Make a hole in your wood block – it has to be big enough for you to be able to wrap string or nylon thread around the dowel when it is inserted later (see photos opposite).
2. Drill a hole horizontally through the large hole (9 mm ($^{23}/_{64}$ in)). This is for the dowel on your spinning top to pass through.
3. Whittle the handle of your wood block so it sits comfortably in your hand, and round off any corners.
4. Push the dowel of the spinning top through the hole and then drill another hole 3.5 mm ($^{9}/_{64}$ in bit) through the dowel. Make sure this hole is exactly in the middle of the dowel (see figure, bottom left).
5. A responsible adult should melt the end of the nylon thread carefully with a lighter or match before cutting it to length; this stops the ends from fraying. Alternatively, you can wind tape around the ends instead.
6. Tie the twig to the end of the string and thread the end through the hole in the dowel.
7. Attach the string to suit either a right-handed or left-handed player, and wind it around the centre of the dowel.
8. Your top is now ready to use. Hold the handle, pull the string (carefully at first, then with more force) and watch it go!

Note: Drilling is a job for a responsible adult. Children should never be allowed to use dangerous tools.

WHITTLED TOP**

Your spinning top doesn't have to be elaborate –you can also create a simple and beautiful top out of a branch, although you will have to work very carefully. For this project, whittle towards your body for more control.

You will need

- Branches, diameter 2.5–3 cm (1–1¼ in), length 10–15 cm (4–6 in)
- Whittling knife
- Saw

How to make it

1. Whittle your branch as shown in the figure (symmetrical so that the top is well balanced later). Make sure the point and the stem are exactly in the centre, and ensure the top has a low centre of gravity.
2. Cut or saw the top off.

Tip: This is a small but tricky project, so be careful. Once you have cut the top from the branch it is difficult to continue whittling, so remember that you will only be able to make fine adjustments afterwards.

ACORN TOP*

This is a small top, but a good, simple project for beginners to make.

You will need

- Acorn with acorn cup (see Figure 1); the acorn should be as symmetrical as possible with its tip in the centre. Acorns of the red oak tree (*quercus rubra*) are best suited, but you can use any variety native to your local area.
- Small twig or piece of wood
- Small drill or screwdriver
- Whittling knife
- Wood glue

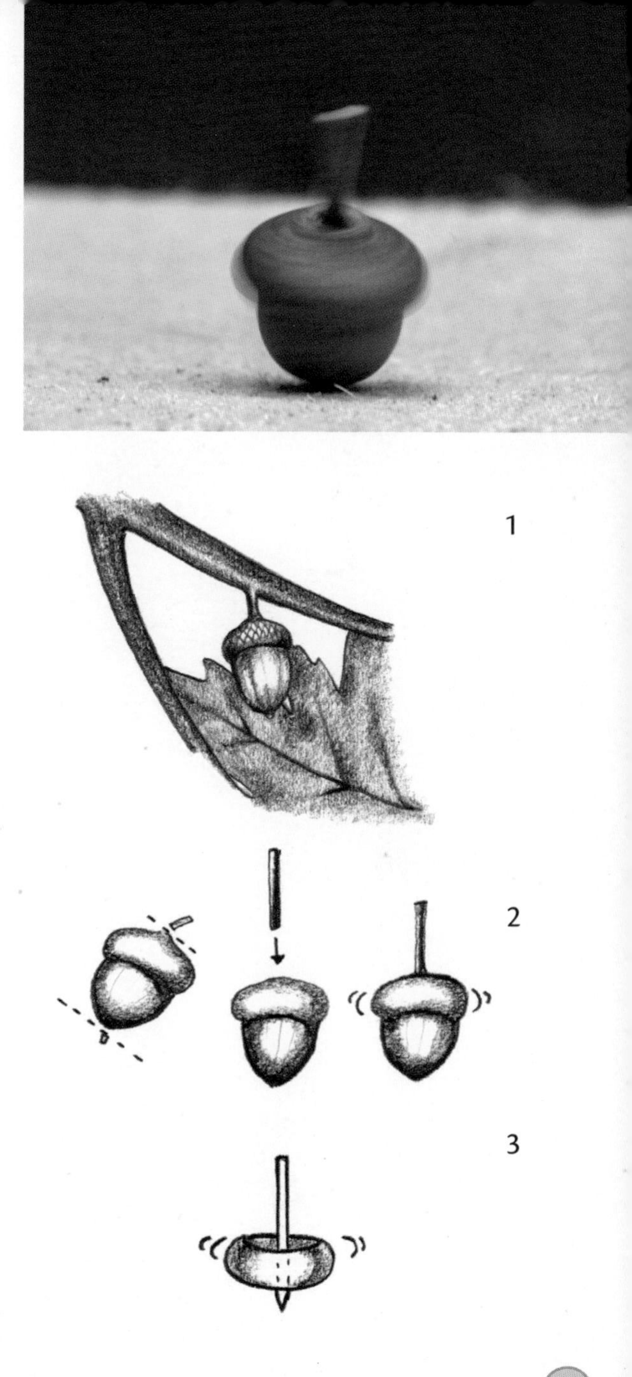

How to make it

1. Using Figure 2 as a guide, cut the acorn cup slightly flat and make a hole in the centre with a small hand drill, electric drill or screwdriver.
2. Glue a small twig or piece of wood into the hole.
3. Carve away a small bit of the acorn point, as it is usually a little uneven and will stop your top from spinning properly.
4. You can also make a top out of the acorn cup. Turn the cup around, drill a hole in it and glue a small piece of wood into it (see Figure 3).

WILLOW BARK FLUTE*

This flute is easier to make than the traditional willow flute as it is made solely out of willow bark and creates a lovely humming sound when played. It is quick to make, but you will only have a limited time to use it – the flute's sound will stop resounding once the bark is dry!

Note: This project can only be made in spring when the bark is green.

You will need

- Willow branch, diameter 5–15 mm (¼–¾ in), length 20–30 cm (8 in–12 in)
- Sharp knife for cutting

How to make it

1. Cut a ring around the bark 6–12 cm (2 ½–5 in) away from the end of the stick (as shown in Figure 1).
2. If necessary, tap along the wood with a thicker branch to loosen the bark (Figure 2), and then carefully slide it off (Figure 3).
3. Cut a single point into one end of the bark (Figure 4).
4. Place the pointed end in your mouth, press the bark together slightly with your lips and blow! Your flute should make a clear humming sound.

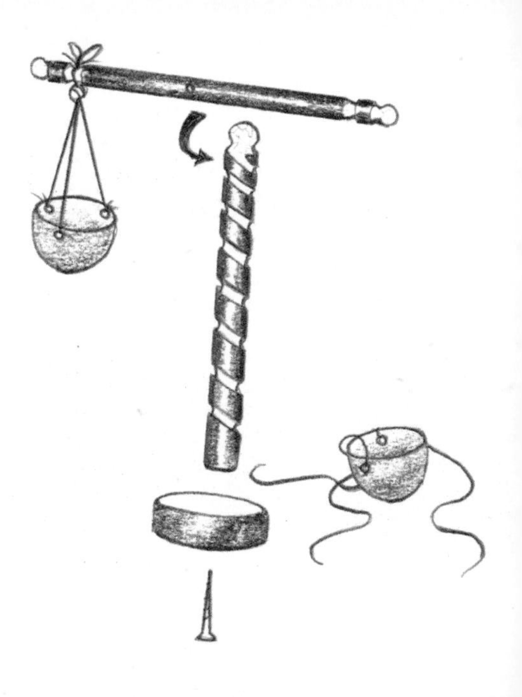

WEIGHING SCALES*

You will need

- Branch 1, diameter 2.5 cm (1 in), length 40 cm (16 in)
- Branch 2, diameter 1.5 cm (¾ in), length 40 cm (16 in)
- Tree slice for the base, diameter 15 cm (6 in)
- Coconut
- Whittling knife
- Sharp knife for cutting (e.g. a kitchen knife)
- 6 strings (e.g. parcel string), each 40 cm (16 in)
- Wood drill, diameter 5 mm (13⁄64 in)
- Screws
- Beeswax (if needed)

Weighing scales are entertaining toys and help children develop a feeling for weight and balance.

Tip: To make the grooves for the string use wood carving technique 2 (see p. 18).

How to make it

1. Branch 1: Round off the top end, and if you'd like to, carve patterns on the branch to add decoration.
2. Screw the branch to the base from below and countersink the screw so that it sits flush with the wood.
3. Branch 2: Whittle a groove around 7 cm (2 ¾ in) in from the ends of the branch for the strings to sit in neatly. Cut 5 cm (2 in) off each end and round them off.
4. Clamp the coconut securely and cut it in half. This isn't easy, so should be a job for a responsible adult. Cut the flesh into triangles and remove using an ordinary kitchen knife.
5. Drill three holes into each coconut half (again, an adult should do this part). Tie a length of string in each hole and knot the string together so the bowl hangs straight.
6. Tie the strings to the crossbar. Find the balancing point by testing it on your finger first, and drill a 5 mm (13⁄64 in bit) hole at this point.
7. Screw the crossbar to Branch 1 using a screw smaller than the hole.
8. If your scales are not perfectly balanced, you can correct them by adding beeswax to the lighter bowl. This will help to balance any small weight differences.

THEATRE WITH FIGURES**

Make your very own puppet theatre, complete with a cast of colourful actors.

You will need

- Blocks of dry lime wood/ basswood, 2.5 x 2.5 x 20 cm (1 x 1 x 8 in) or branch, diameter 2.5–3 cm (1–1 ¼ in)
- Whittling knife
- Paint or pencils for decoration
- Scraps of fabric, leather and wool

How to make it

1. Carve the head of the figure from your block of wood. Draw a rough outline of the shape first as a guide if it helps.
2. Make sure you position the head so the nose is at a corner of the wood block; this makes it easier to whittle a nose that will stick out.
3. Whittle a narrow neck and a round body to fit comfortably in your hand.
4. Add a face with paint or coloured pencils.
5. Use scraps of fabric and leather to make clothes, hats, hair and even beards!

A SMALL THEATRE*

The easiest theatre to make is a piece of fabric fastened in a doorway (as shown in the illustration below). However, a picture frame can also make an attractive theatre front.

You will need

- Picture frame
- Wooden box (same size as your picture frame)
- Clamps (if necessary)
- Fabric for curtains

How to make it

1. Attach the frame to a wooden box of the same size. This should make a box with a window in the front.
2. Place the frame on the edge of a table and secure with clamps if necessary.
3. Use your fabric to make curtains and attach them to the frame.

SOUND STICKS*

You will need

- 2 branches, diameter 2.5 cm (1 in), length 15 cm (6 in). Hazel is good as it is easy to carve a pattern in the bark and the wood resonates well when dry.
- Whittling knife

How to make it

1. Remove the bark from one end of the branches, leaving enough bark at the other to grip the sticks.
2. Carefully round off the ends of the sticks.
3. If you like, you can also carve beautiful patterns into the grip-ends.

BUILDING BLOCKS*

You will need

- Fresh branches, diameter 2.5–4 cm (1–1 ½ in) (long enough to hold while whittling)
- Whittling knife
- Saw
- Linseed oil (optional)

How to make it

Branch blocks:

1. Round off the ends of your branches.
2. If you want to, you can make your blocks more decorative by whittling patterns in the bark (as seen in the photo on the left).
3. Saw the block to the size you want, making sure the base is straight enough to be stacked.

Flat blocks or "walkways":

1. Split the branch (see p. 23 and figure below).
2. Round off the edges of the branch.
3. If you want to, apply linseed oil to the flat areas for a smooth, tactile finish.

Towers:

1. Whittle one end of the branch into a point.
2. Saw the tower to the desired length.
3. Again, if you want, apply linseed oil to the whittled areas.
4. You can add a flag to your towers using a small rectangle of coloured paper attached to a twig or piece of dowel. Fix it to the top of your tower with wood glue.

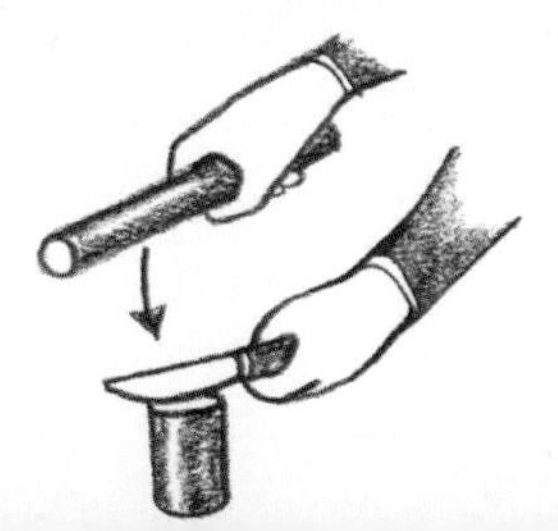

WOODLAND LANDSCAPE*

You will need

- Shoebox
- Coloured paper or gift wrap
- Cotton wool, carded wool or silk
- Glue stick
- Wood shavings, needle and thread
- Paint
- Leather, fabric or wool
- Whittled figures

How to make it

Landscape:

1. Cover the shoebox with coloured paper.
2. To make the stars, glue small wood shavings or triangles of white paper over each other.
3. Tie or glue a thread to the stars and secure to the roof of the box with a needle.
4. Make a knot in the thread so the stars hang down, and cut off the thread, or attach with sticky tape.
5. Place cotton wool, white wool or silk over the ground. Secure with glue if you want.
6. Add small fir twigs to act as trees.

Gnome with hair:

1. Follow the steps of the "Bird with a feathery tail " project on p. 33 and whittle the hair in the same way.
2. Make the gnome's hat out of a piece of leather or fabric, or use a knitted hat.
3. Paint or decorate however you like, but make sure to add some rosy cheeks!

Reindeer:

1. Make a reindeer in the same way you made the pigs and dogs on p. 40.
2. Make the antlers out of small twigs and secure them with glue.

BALL-IN-A-CAGE RATTLE***

This project is a little more difficult, and requires lots of care and patience. For guidance, if you are making a rattle with a ball for the first time, it's best to use a square block in the size given for ease.

You will need

- Dry lime wood (basswood) block, 3.5 x 3.5 x 22 cm (1½ x 1½ x 8¾ in)
- Drill, diameter 16–18 mm (⅝–²³⁄₃₂ in)
- Chisel
- Whittling knife with a sharp point
- Protective glove
- Linseed oil

How to make it

1. Sketch the ball on your block of wood, diameter 3 cm (1 ¼ in).
2. Drill holes on both sides of the ball and connect the holes with two lines to mark the place where you need to remove the wood. Make a groove along the line with the chisel (see Figure 1).
3. Shape the ball with the chisel from all four sides without taking wood away from the four "bars" (see Figures 2 and 3).

1

2

3

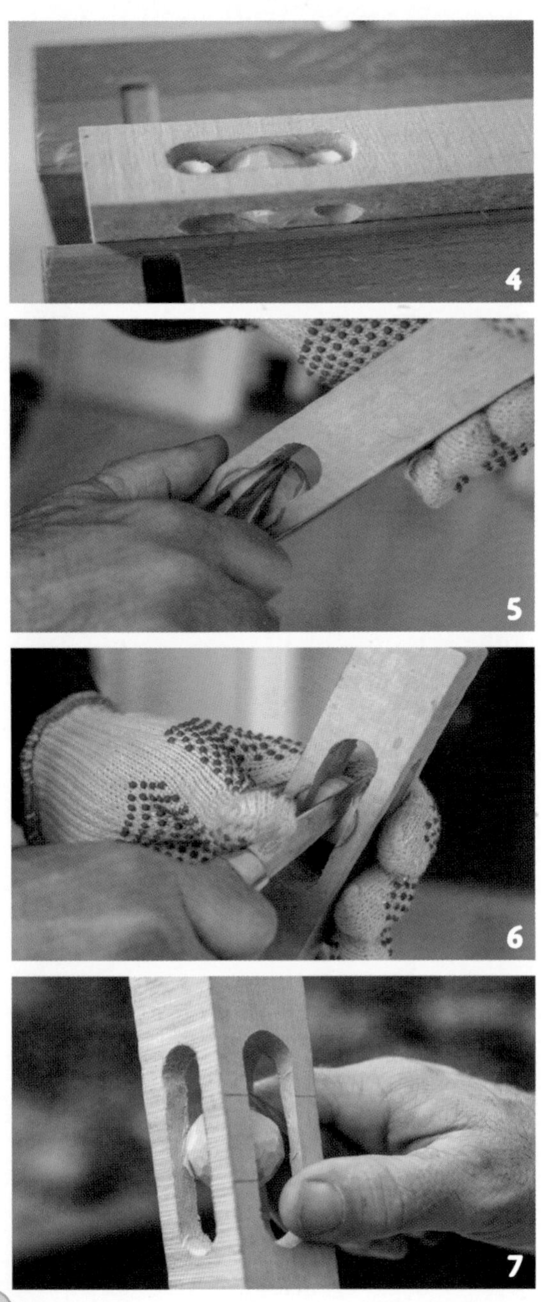

4. Once the ball has a basic outline (Figure 4), continue to shape the ball with the whittling knife (Figures 5 and 6). It is safer to use a glove for this part. Carefully whittle the ball round and slightly smaller. There are two techniques you can use here:
   - Hold the knife and cut towards your thumb, which is protected by the "bar" (Figure 5).
   - Control the knife with your thumb (the thumb push technique, Figure 6).
5. Carefully carve away some of the inside of the "bar" to make space for the ball. Keep rounding off the ball.
6. Carefully continue working until the ball breaks free from one of the "bars" (Figure 7), then whittle the ball free from the opposite "bar". Leave the ball attached to the remaining "bars" and continue rounding it off. Note that once the ball is completely free it is difficult to continue whittling.
7. Whittle the rest of the rattle with any decoration you would like to add (see photo on p. 76).
8. Apply linseed oil with a paintbrush.

Tip: You can also make a bird, with a loose egg inside it instead of a rattle, as shown in the photo on the right.

SKIER AND DRUMMER***

This is a fun toy that works with the movement of your hands: the weight swings back and forth, causing the figure's arms to move up and down. It is best to make the drummer using fresh branches and the skier out of dry lime wood (basswood), but you can use different materials if you want to.

You will need (both)

- Wood for holding piece, 1 x 4.5 x 23 cm (½ x 1¾ x 9 in)
- Branch for the weight, for example diameter 2 cm (1 in), length 8 cm (3 in); you can also use a shorter and thicker piece or a whittled ball, see the photo of the skier on p. 83.
- Thin round sticks for drumsticks or ski poles, diameter approx. 3 mm (just under ¼ in), e.g. bamboo skewers
- Whittling knife
- Drill
- Small nails
- Wood glue
- Strong thread or string

SKIER***

You will need

- Dry lime wood (basswood), 2.5 x 3.5 x 10 cm (1 x 1½ x 4 in)
- Dry lime wood (basswood) for the arms, 1 cm (½ in) thick
- Branch for the skis, diameter 1–2 cm (½–2 in), length 11 cm (4 ½ in), preferably with a small curve at the end so the skis bend up at the tip
- Saw
- Scraps of leather

How to make it

1. Sketch the outline of your skier on the wood (see the figure below for shape).
2. Whittle the figure and arms; saw them out first if necessary.
3. Split the branch for the skis, whittle flat "boards" and glue them under the skier.
4. Follow the further steps for both on p. 83.

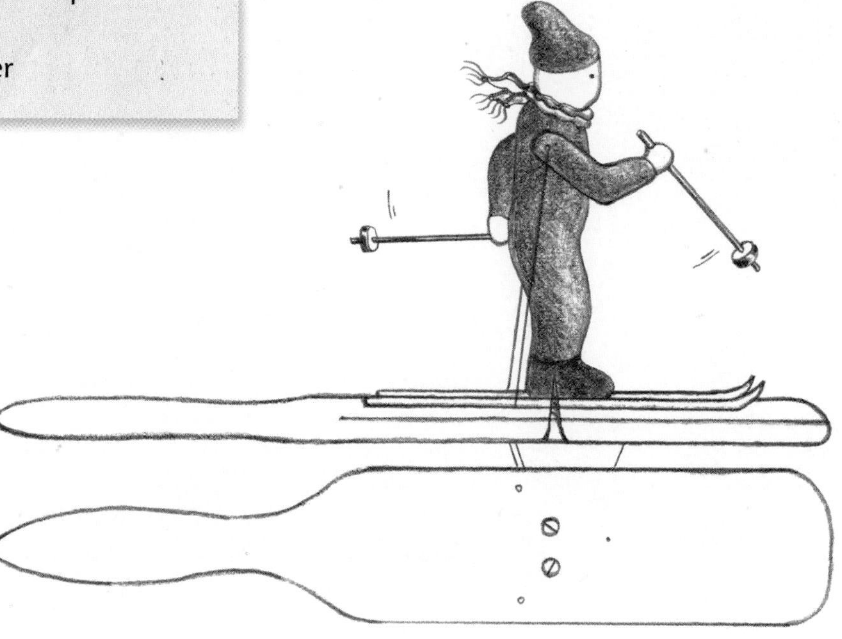

DRUMMER***

You will need

- Branch, diameter 2.5 cm (1 in), length 10 cm (4 in)
- Branches for the arms, diameter 1.5 cm (½ in), length 4.5 cm (1¾ in)
- 2 small wood beads or similar for the head of the drumsticks
- Branch for the drum, diameter 3 cm (1¼ in), length 3 cm (1¼ in)

How to make it

1. Sketch the outline of your drummer on the branch.
2. Carve the entire figure including the head.
3. Split the branch for the arms and whittle them.
4. Follow the further steps opposite.

2

1

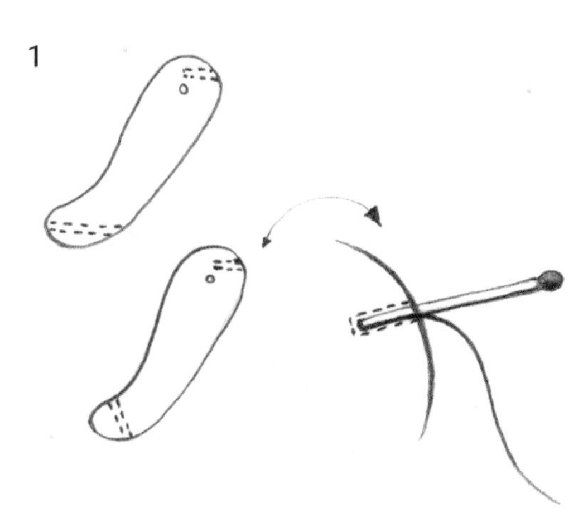

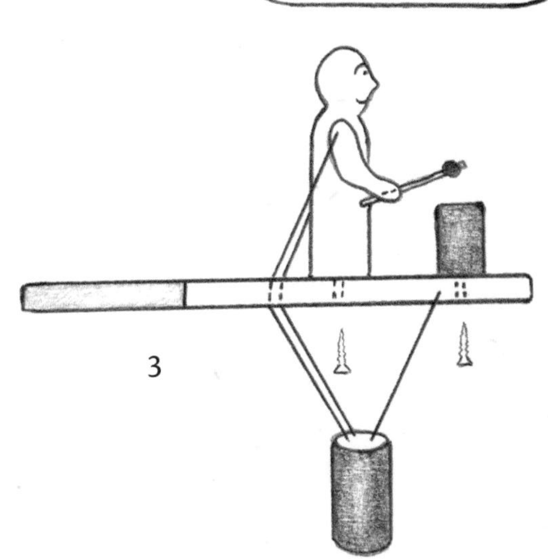

3

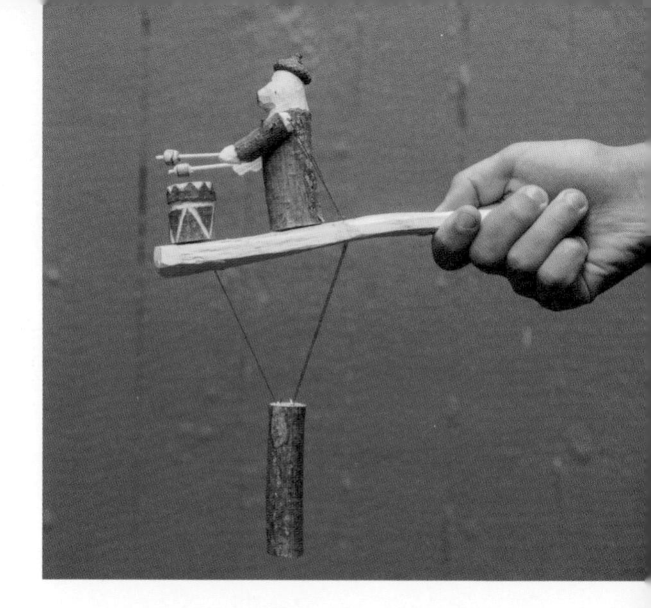

Further steps for skier and drummer

1. Drill 2 mm ($\frac{5}{64}$ in bit) holes in the arms for nails, then push (see Figure 1) and glue the thread into the holes.
2. Drill holes in the hands for the ski poles or drumsticks. See Figure 3 (drummer) and p. 81 (skier) for the correct angle.
3. Attach small round leather pieces to the ski poles or small wood beads to the drumsticks. Push or glue them into the hand holes.
4. Whittle the holding piece (saw it out first if you'd like to).
5. Place the figure on the holding piece, mark and drill holes for the arm threads (see Figure 2). Glue or screw the figure and drum in place.
6. Drill three holes for the threads into the wood weight and drill a hole from below into the holding piece. Sometimes you won't need this hole in the holding piece, which leaves only two holes for the arm threads in the weight. The wood under the holding piece needs a certain weight so the arms will swing, but it can't be too heavy or the arms will stay up. If necessary, saw it to a smaller size after it is attached.
7. Thread the two arm strings through the two holes in the holding piece and together with the string from under the holding piece, attach to the "weight" below (see Figure 3). Be careful to make both arm threads the same length or the toy won't work.
8. Push the thread into the armholes and wedge in place with a sliver of wood (see Figure 1), then glue tight.

1
2
3
4

JACK IN THE BOX**

Pull the thread and Jack will jump out of the box. Surprise!

You will need

- Branch, diameter 4–5 cm (1½–2 in), length 10–15 cm (4–6 in). It is best to use dry wood.
- Wood for the figure, diameter slightly smaller than the drilled hole and as long as the depth of the hole, preferably slightly longer
- Drill, different diameters 20–30 mm ($^{25}/_{32}$–1$^{3}/_{16}$ in), 2–3 mm ($^{1}/_{8}$ in) and 5 mm ($^{13}/_{64}$ in)
- Whittling knife
- Wood glue
- Length of thin wire
- Matchstick
- String or strong thread
- Bead or small piece of wood for the handle
- Paint for decoration

How to make it

1. Drill a deep hole in the branch for Jack to pop out of, diameter 20–30 mm ($^{25}/_{32}$–1$^{3}/_{16}$ in bit).
2. Whittle the figure, as well as a groove for the string (see Figure 1).
3. Drill a hole in the figure, 2–3 mm ($^{1}/_{8}$ in bit) in diameter for the string, apply glue and wedge the string in place with a matchstick (see Figure 2). Break off the excess matchstick length.
4. Drill a hole in the branch wood for the string, diameter 5 mm ($^{13}/_{64}$ in bit). The position of this hole determines how high Jack will pop.
5. Push a doubled length of thin wire through the hole to feed the string through, and pull the string out when it appears. Check whether Jack jumps.
6. Tie a bead or a small piece of wood to the string as a handle (if you whittle a groove in the centre of the wood first then string will hold better).
7. Don't forget to paint Jack!

Tips: If the figure doesn't move back down easily after popping up either the figure or the hole are too angular.

If the figure is standing squint or gets caught, then either the hole for the thread is too high up or the figure is too thin in relation to the hole.

It can help to increase the figure's weight to encourage it to move up and down. You can do this by inserting a screw into it from below.

SEESAW TOY***

Toys with a seesaw motion are great fun. You can either copy the models shown here or make up your own versions!

The seesaw effect is produced by alternately pushing and pulling the horizontal slats. The instructions here are based on two figures, but you can also make toys with more, for example the family of four bears in the top left photo.

You will need (seesaw)

- 2 wood slats, 8 x 21 mm (½ x 1 in), or a branch split or sawn in half lengthways, diameter 3–3.5 cm (1¼–1 ½ in), length 25–30 cm (10–12 in)
- Drill, diameter 2 mm, 8 mm and 9 mm (5/64, 5/16 and 23/64 in)
- Whittling knife
- 4 thin nails, length 2 cm (1 in) – the nails may need to be longer for a split branch
- Hammer
- Dowels, diameter 8 mm (½ in), length 8 cm (3¼ in)
- Wood glue

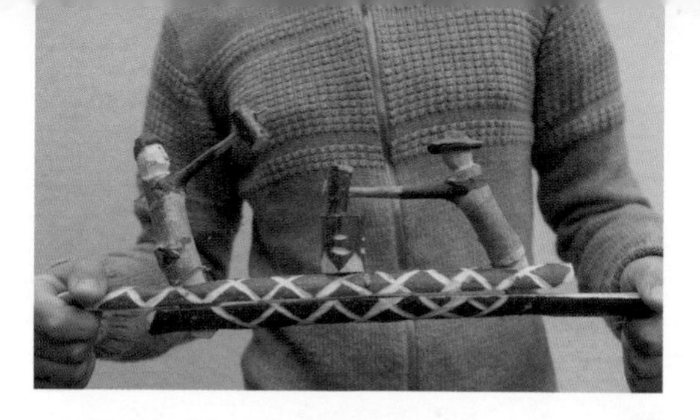

You will need (birds)

- Branches, diameter 2.5–3 cm (1–1¼ in), length 20 cm (8 in)
- To make the birds pulling at a worm (see photo above), you will need a length of leather cord or similar
- Whittling knife
- Paint for decoration

How to make it (bird)

1. Whittle the bird (see instructions for "Bird made from a single branch" on p. 31).
2. Drill an 8 mm (5⁄16 in bit) hole from below, about halfway into the bird, and push a dowel in to the hole.
3. If you want the bird to pull at a worm later, drill a hole in the beak for the string.
4. Paint or decorate your birds.

You will need (men)

- Branch with side branch (see Figure 2 over page), diameter of main branch 2.5–3 cm (1–1¼ in), length 14 cm (5½ in)
- Whittling knife
- Paint for decoration
- Branches for the axes and chopping block (for woodcutter men)
- String (for men pulling rope)

How to make it (men)

1. Whittle the head of your man and cut the side branch to arm length (if you want your men to be chopping wood, remember the additional axe length, drill a hole in the axe head and push it on the arm piece).
2. Whittle a peg on the lower end of the figure for attaching to the slat. Alternatively, saw the figure to the desired length, drill a hole from below and push a dowel into the hole.
3. Paint or decorate your man.

The seesaw mechanism:

1. Position the figures according to their activity (e.g. chopping wood, pulling rope) and mark where to drill the holes on the wood slats. For example, make sure the woodcutter men actually hit the chopping block with their axes.
2. Drill four 9 mm (23/64 in bit) holes in each wood slat. The distance between the holes should be approx. 2 cm (1 in) (see Figure 3).
3. Remove the wood between the holes with your whittling knife and drill a 2 mm (5/64 in bit) hole from the side (see Figure 4).
4. If you are making the birds pulling at a worm design, drill two holes and feed a length of string through (see Figure 5).
5. Push the figures into the oval shaped holes of the upper slat, not too far in so they can still seesaw back and forth.
6. Hold them in place and mark the dowel for drilling the hole with a sharp nail. Remove the figure again and drill a 2 mm (5/64 in bit) hole in the dowel (see Figure 6).
7. Push the figure back in the long hole again and nail in place (see Figure 7). Don't hammer the nail in completely at first in case it needs readjusting.
8. Attach the dowel on the other side in the same way, but remember to keep around 3 mm (just under ¼ in) distance between the two slats.

Men with a rope:

1. Cut a length of string to the appropriate length, pull it tight between the men's hands and glue in place.

Men with axes:

1. Drill a hole in the bottom of the chopping block and top of the upper slat and connect with a dowel. If you need to, glue it in place (see Figure 8).

Tip: If you make a toy with more than two figures, check whether the seesaw mechanism works with only two figures attached first, then add the others afterwards.

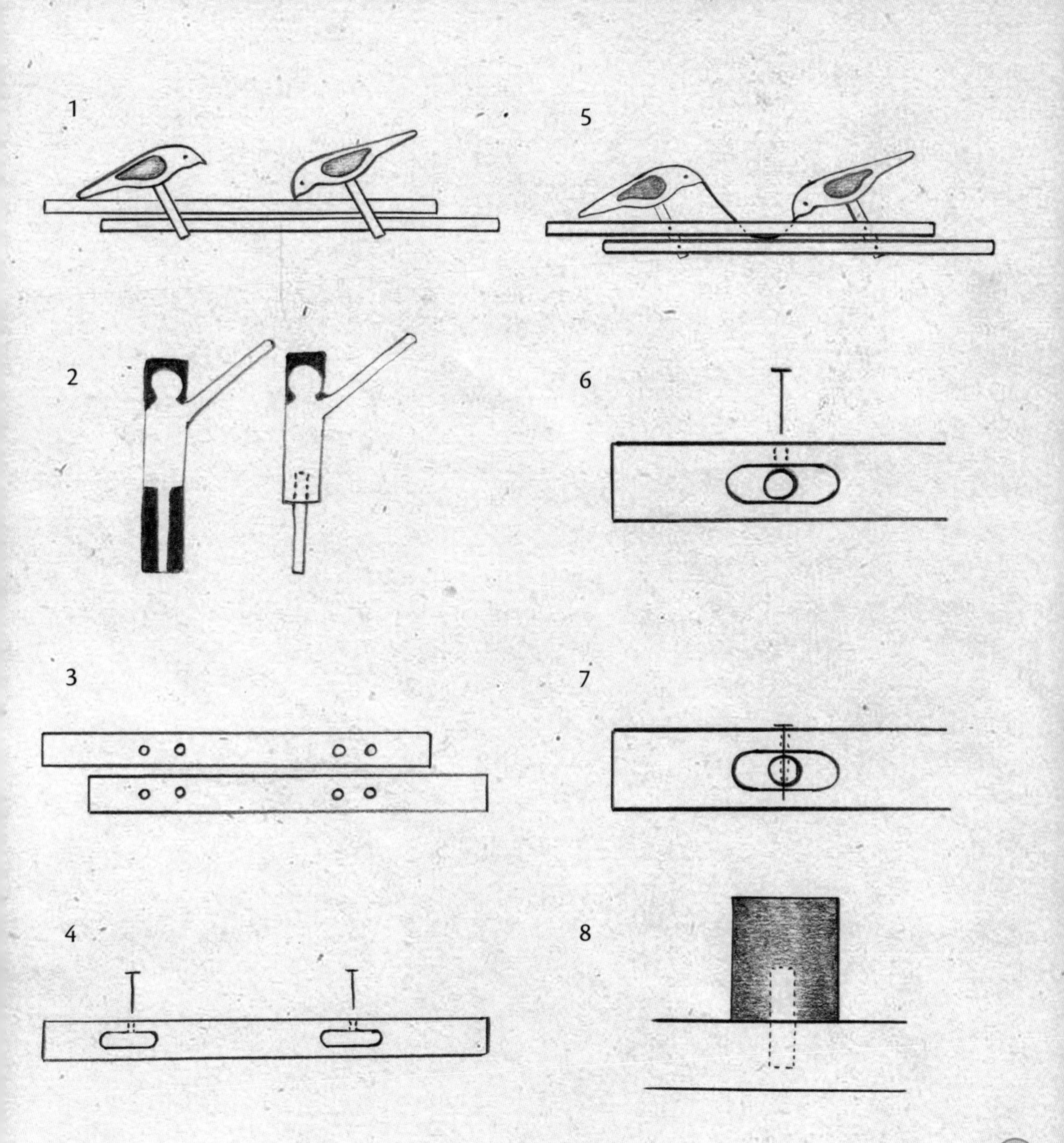
1
2
3
4
5
6
7
8

JEWELLERY

SLIDING ADJUSTABLE KNOT**

This isn't technically a whittling activity, but it will come in useful for the other jewellery projects in this section. Learning how to make sliding adjustable knots is a helpful skill, and means that you can adjust your necklaces to any length.

You will need

- Leather cord, approx. one and a half times as long as the circumference of your head (it is best to use a thin cord so it breaks if it gets caught)
- A pendant (you can practise with a pendant from an existing necklace if you haven't learnt to make your own yet)

How to make it

1. Thread your pendant on the cord and tie one end of the cord as shown in Figures 1, 2 and 3.
2. Turn the cord around and repeat with the other end (see Figures 4 and 5).
3. Pull the knots apart and the pendant will be tighter (see Figure 6), be sure to leave some excess cord at each end of the knot for pulling.
4. If you want to take it off, push the knots together so you can slide the necklace back over your head.

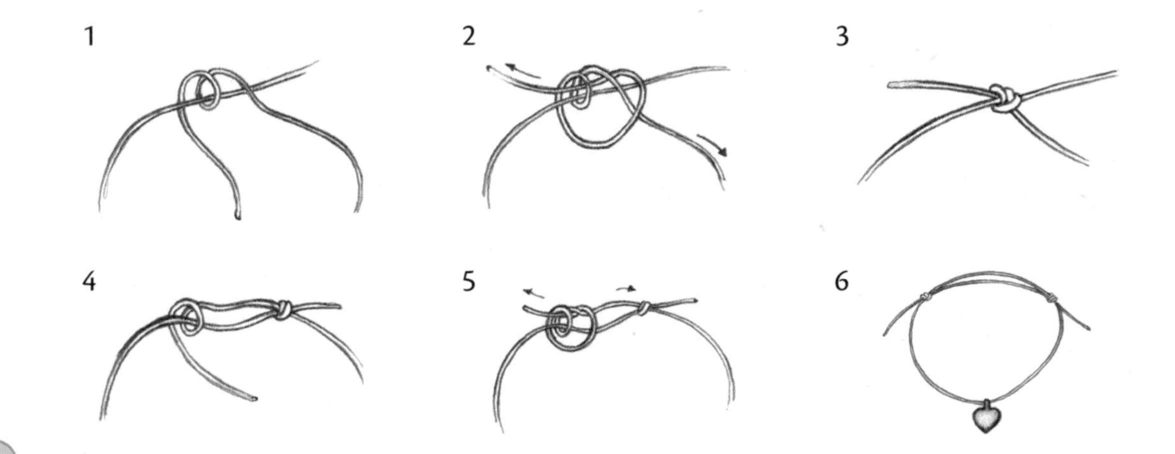

HEART PENDANT**

This is a nice project for a practised and patient wood carving master!

You will need

- Small block of wood, for example 1.5 x 3 x 10 cm (¾ x 1¼ x 4 in)
- Whittling knife
- Drill, diameter 2 mm (5⁄64 in)
- Sandpaper
- Saw
- Linseed oil
- Length of leather cord

How to make it

1. As shown in the figure, carve or saw a peg at the top of your piece of wood and round it off. This will sit at the top of your heart.
2. Drill a 2 mm (5⁄64 in) hole through the peg for threading a necklace through.
3. Whittle the heart and only then cut or saw the peg to the desired length.
4. Continue shaping the heart, then sand it.
5. Apply linseed oil to make the heart "glow".

6. Thread a length of leather cord through the hole in the peg and secure using a sliding adjustable knot (see opposite).

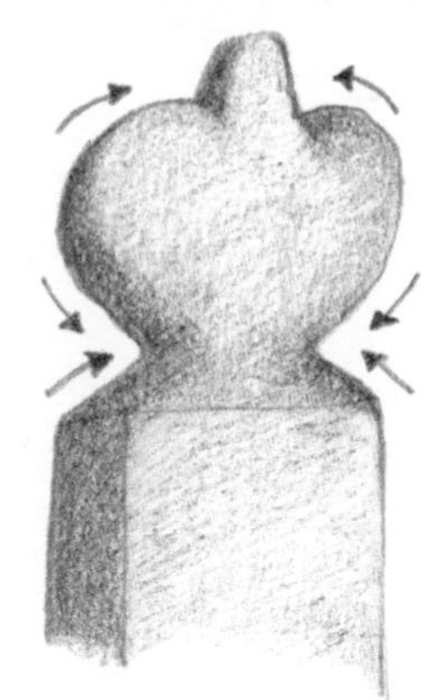

SWORD PENDANT**

A sword pendant makes a good amulet to help you win battles!

You will need

- Small block of dry wood, for example 1 x 2 cm (½ x 1 in), length 10–12 cm (4–5 in); you can also split a branch to 4.5 mm (approx. ¼ in) (see figure below, the marked section is your work piece) or use a smaller branch
- Whittling knife
- Drill, diameter 2 mm ($\frac{5}{64}$ in)
- Sandpaper (optional)
- Paints for decoration (optional)
- Length of leather cord

How to make it

1. First whittle the sword's cross-guard (see the arrows on the figure below for carving directions). Work carefully so you don't break it off.
2. Whittle the blade to a point and finish with the hilt.
3. Drill a 2 mm ($\frac{5}{64}$ in bit) hole through the hilt.
4. If you want to, sand the sword and paint it.
5. Pull a thin leather cord through the hole and secure with a sliding adjustable knot (see p. 92).

Tip: You can also make the sword out of a small branch with two side branches opposite each other (see the photo opposite).

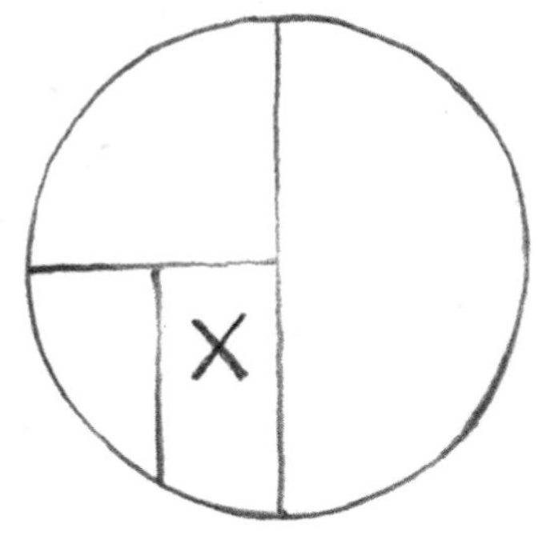

DOLPHIN PENDANT OR EARRING**

Dolphins are clever and playful – they make good friends and are nice to wear as jewellery.

You will need

- Small branch with side branch
- Whittling knife
- Thin metal ring (you can make this yourself by winding a length of wire around a screwdriver or a large nail and cutting the ends)
- Drill with small bit
- Sandpaper
- Length of leather cord
- Earring (optional)
- Paint for decoration (optional)

How to make it

1. Carve the dolphin (see p. 43 for full instructions).
2. Carefully drill a small hole in the dorsal fin, large enough to fit a metal ring for a necklace, or a hook for an earring.
3. Sand the surface smooth.
4. If you want to, paint your dolphin.
5. Attach the ring to the hole and thread a piece of leather cord through, securing with a sliding adjustable knot (see p. 92). Alternatively, if you're making an earring, use the hole to attach the dolphin to the earring.

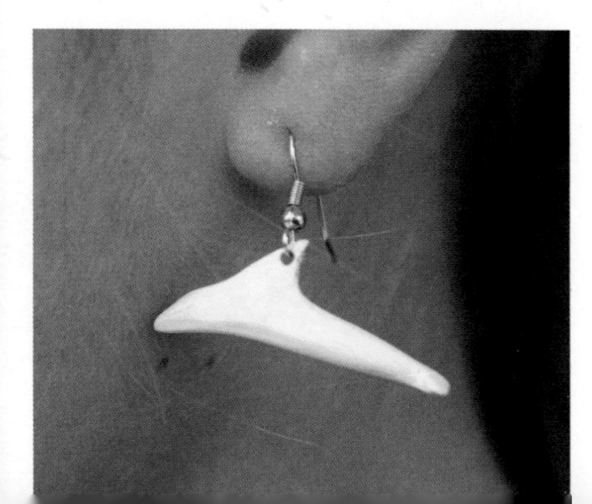

MINIATURE RATTLE PENDANT***

Making a miniature rattle as jewellery is something of a challenge for any whittler. You will need experience, care and patience. If you have these and a small sharp whittling knife you can look forward to many hours of creative work! It's best to make the large rattle before attempting this smaller trickier project (see p. 77 for details).

You will need

- Dry wood (the rattles in the photos are yew, but be careful – yew berries and needles are poisonous!);
  2 x 2 cm (1 x 1 in) or slightly larger, length 12 cm (5 in)
- Whittling knife
- Drill, diameter 5 mm (13/64 in)
- Sandpaper
- Linseed oil
- Length of leather cord

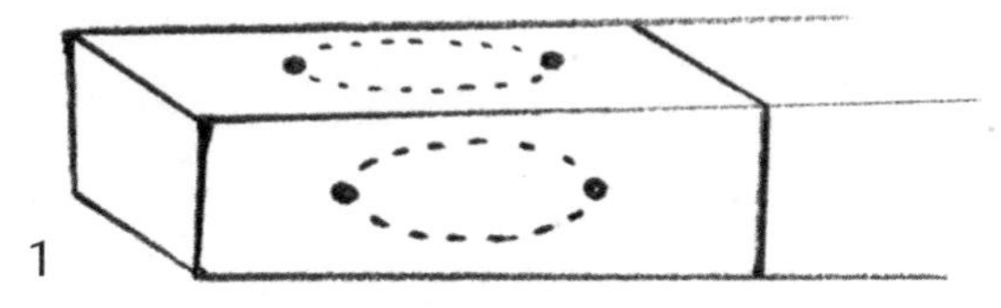

How to make it

1. See instructions for "Ball-in-a-cage rattle" on p. 77, but only use your whittling knife, not a chisel.
2. Drill four holes and then carve oval holes out of them (see Figure 1). Work with fine, small cuts; a single incorrect cut can ruin the entire project.
3. Drill a hole for the leather string, sand the rattle and apply oil.
4. Pull a piece of thin leather cord through the hole and secure with a sliding adjustable knot (see p. 92).

Note: For size guidance, the rattles shown in the photos are 5–8 cm (2–3 in) long.

PARSLEY
BEETROOT
CARROT

HOME AND GARDEN

CARROT
BEETROOT

PLANT LABELS**

Plant labels help to organise any garden or allotment. Draw a picture on your label of what you're growing or whittle the top into a shape for added decoration.

You will need

- Branches (e.g. hazel), as long as you need for labelling
- Whittling knife
- Waterproof ink and paint

How to make it

1. Whittle a good long point on one end of a branch to insert into the ground (see Figure 1).
2. Carve the other end flat so you can write or paint on it (see Figure 2). If you like, you can whittle the top of the label into the shape of a plant or vegetable, like those seen in the photos opposite.
3. Write the name of the vegetable with waterproof ink, and decorate with waterproof paint.

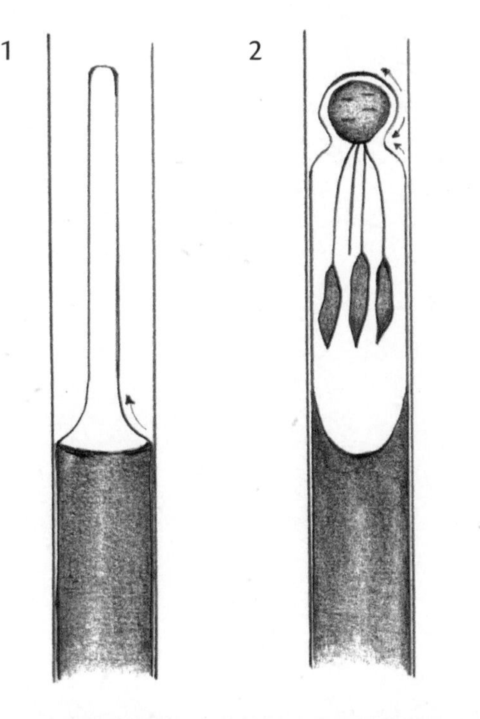

STARS**

You will need

- Branch, diameter 8–20 mm (approx. ½–1 in)
- Thin metal wire, 10–20 cm (4–8 in)
- Drill, 1.5 mm (1⁄16 in)
- Whittling knife
- Wood glue
- Needle and thread for hanging up (optional)

How to make it

1. Split the branch to make four narrow slats and smooth any uneven parts with the whittling knife. The slats should all roughly be the same length (8–15 cm (3¼–6 in)).
2. Cut both ends of the slats into a point and drill a hole into the centre of each.
3. Fold the wire in half and twist a few times to make a small ring.
4. Arrange the four slats into a star, apply wood glue to the centre and push the wire through the holes.
5. Pull the ends of the wire apart so all four wood pieces are firmly connected (see figure, below). You can use the wire to attach the star to something else, for example, a Christmas tree.
6. If you would rather hang up your star, drill a small hole in one of the tips and insert a thread, using a needle if needed.

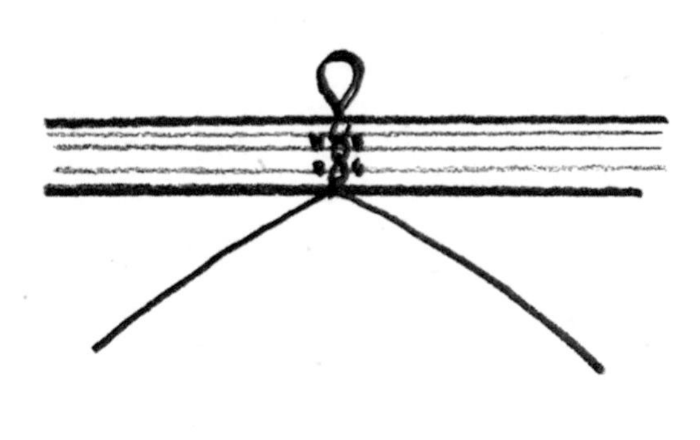

FRIENDLY WILL-O'-THE-WISPS*

The Chinese lantern flower (*Physalis alkekengi*) grows like a weed in some gardens, but it has a beautiful, fiery coloured flower that makes the perfect hat for a friendly will-o'-the-wisp.

You will need

- Branch
- Whittling knife
- Ink
- Wood glue
- Chinese lantern flower

How to make it

1. Take your branch and remove one or two shavings of bark for the face with your whittling knife.
2. Draw a mouth and some eyes with ink (remember to make your will-o'-the-wisp look friendly!) and cut the branch to the size you would like.
3. Gently position the Chinese lantern flower on the top of your branch, and secure with a spot of wood glue. Hold it briefly so it stays in place, but take care, it's easy to squash!

FIR TREE**

You will need

- Whittling knife
- Saw
- Paint for decoration (optional)

Fir trees with grooves

- Branch, diameter 3–4 cm (1¼–1½ in) or dry lime wood (basswood) 1 x 3 cm (½ x 1¼ in)

Fir tree with cuts or wood shavings

- Branch, diameter 2–4 cm (1–1½ in)

There are three different types of fir trees shown here:

1. With grooves (see Figure 1)
2. With cuts (see Figure 2)
3. With wood shavings (see Figures 3 and 4). This type is much more difficult (***), so only attempt it if you have used this technique before.

How to make it

Fir with grooves:

1. Whittle a point, then narrow two opposite sides for the grooves. You can use an axe to roughly shape your tree first.
2. Carve grooves along the edges – take care the tips don't break off.

Fir tree with cuts:

1. Whittle a rough cone shape. You can whittle the piece round, square, five-sided or six-sided.
2. Cut into the branch starting at the top and work your way around.
3. Place the cuts roughly equally distanced and exactly below each other.

Tip: A small grooved fir tree makes a nice gift tag (see photo on p. 122).

Fir tree with curled shavings:

1. Take a branch and make a point at one end. You can carve it into a round or square shape.
2. Let the branch dry for a couple of days before whittling the curls. Starting at the top, carefully whittle curls around the branch. The curls of the next round should be exactly below the ones above.
3. You can make the curls longer with each round, ending at the bottom with the longest curls.

For all types:

1. Saw the finished tree to the correct length.
2. You can paint your tree if you want to, but note that the curls may unfurl when wet.

Tip: You can also use a larger branch, whittle it narrower and then make the curls on two opposite sides.

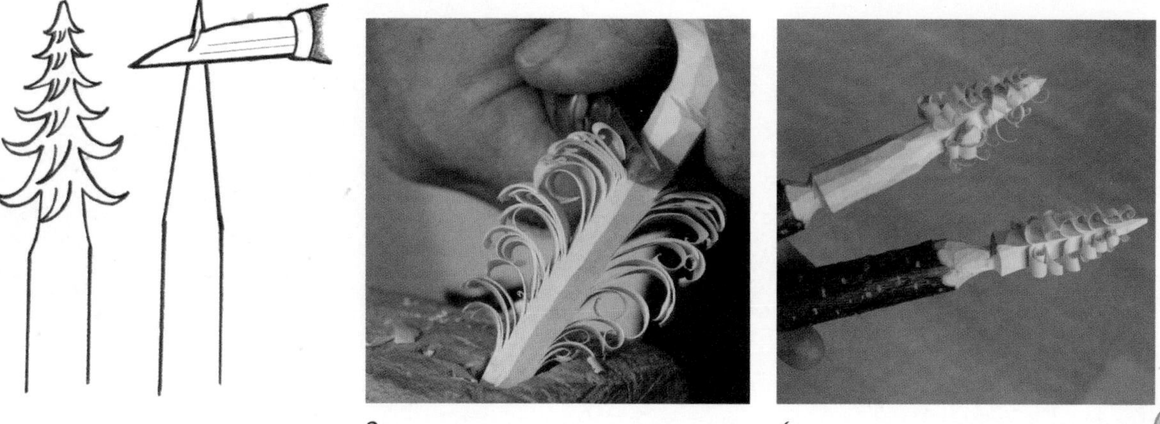

2 3 4

PICTURE FRAME**

You can make a simple and decorative picture frame out of just a few branches. For a more advanced task, making a triangular or curved branch frame can be quite a challenge (see middle photo below).

Note: Sizes are for example only. Your picture frame can be as big or small as you like.

You will need

- 4 branches, diameter 2.5 cm (1 in), length (2 pieces) 20 cm (8 in), (2 pieces) 25 cm (10 in)
- Whittling knife
- Saw
- Wood glue or small nails/screws
- Hammer
- Tape or clips

How to make it

1. Whittle away around one fifth of the branch to make a flat back for the frame.
2. Make a notch on the front side of one of the branches, length the same as the diameter of the corresponding branch piece (see photo). To do this, saw two parallel cuts approx. halfway through the branch and remove the wood between the cuts with a chisel or whittling knife. Make a notch on the back of the corresponding branch. Prepare the four branches for assembly in this way.
3. If you want to, carve patterns in the bark and round the ends to decorate.
4. Once you have prepared the branches, place the notches over each other and connect with wood glue or small nails or screws. Hammer in the nails or screw screws from the back.
5. Attach the picture from the back of the frame with tape or clips.

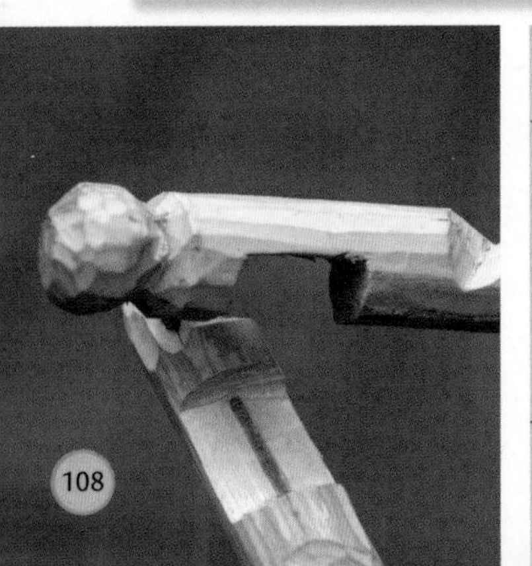

STRAW FLOWERS***

A colourful bunch of whittled flowers makes a great gift. The difficulty of this project lies in carving thin shavings without them breaking off.

You will need

- Branch (elder is good), diameter 1–2 cm (½–1 in), length 10–20 cm (4–8 in), fresh branches with too much soft pith in the centre are not suited
- Thin branch or twig for the stem
- Whittling knife
- Wood stain or watercolour paint

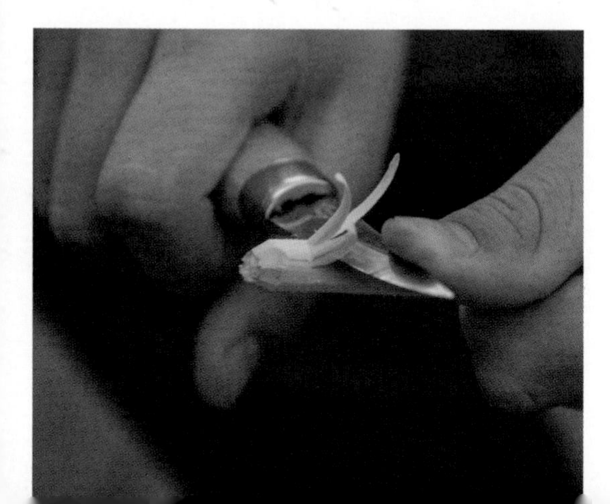

How to make it

1. Whittle or scrape off the bark from your branch approx. 6–8 cm (2½–3¼ in) and round off one end.
2. Whittle a long, thin shaving, around 2.5–5 cm (1–2 in), stopping 1 cm (½ in) before the end. You can use carving technique 2 on p. 18 (see photo on previous page).
3. If you need to, lift the shaving up a little as you work, and cut more shavings around the branch and then below the first row. Be careful not to cut too deep or the flower will break off. Too many small cuts into the centre of the branch will also result in the flower breaking.
4. Press the twig for your stem into the pith of your whittled flower.
5. Colour the flowers by immersing them completely in paint. You can then add different hues with a paintbrush by covering the entire flower in yellow and then painting the shaving tips with red.

1

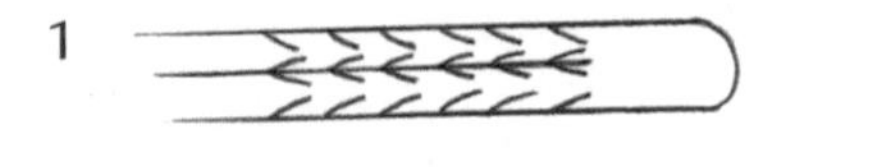

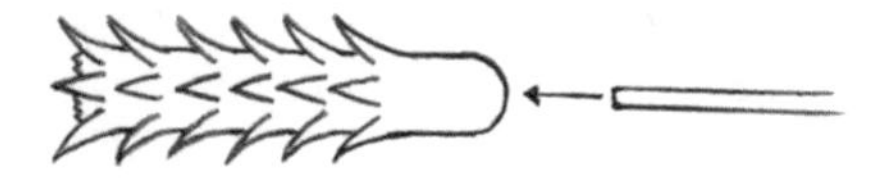

2

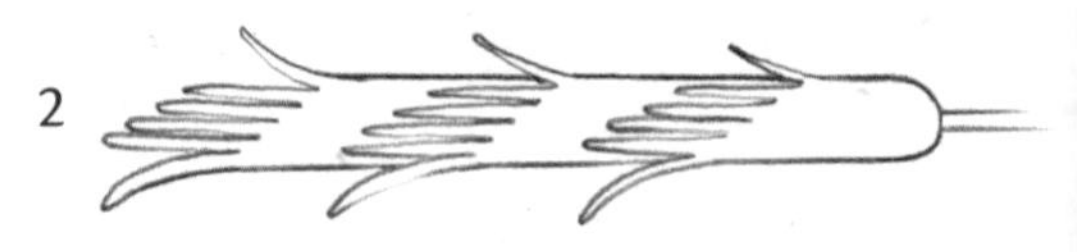

3

Flower variations

Grain head:

Whittle three, four or even five sides and make small cuts into the edges (see Figure 1).

Elongated flower:

Carve the shavings into a spiral around the flower (see Figure 2).

Curled petals:

Strip the bark from the branch and let the branch dry. The fine shavings will curl like plane curls (see Figure 3). Don't immerse this model in wood stain or paint as the petals will straighten out if they get wet.

Flower with pistil:

First whittle petals around the outside so the pistil remains standing in the centre, then carve grooves around its edge (see Figure 4).

Flower with narrow and wide petals:

Whittle five sides. Cut narrow petals into the edges first, and then wider petals to finish the pistil (see Figure 5). Paint the narrow petals with a paintbrush and green paint.

Small flowers with stem:

Attach small whittled flowers to a straight or y-shaped branch (see photo below).

4

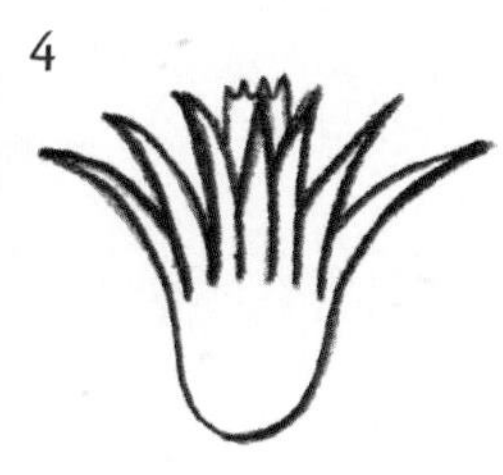

5

WHITTLING BARK*

You will need

- Thick piece of bark, for example spruce bark, or a piece of bark chip
- Whittling knife

With its beautiful colours and picturesque structures, bark is a fascinating material to work with. It's very soft and great for wood carving, but can be a little tricky as the different layers can come apart.

However, bark is very versatile and can easily be used to make jewellery, animals, boats, houses and lots of other decorative objects.

PULLED FIBRE BROOM**

This decorative Native American brush from Wisconsin and Minnesota is made out of a single branch. To get the best results, whittle towards your body when making this project.

You will need

- Branch without knots, twisted grain or side branches, diameter 3–4 cm (1¼–1½ in), length 35 cm (14 in). It is best to use hazel or birch if possible.
- Whittling knife
- Willow twig, leather thong or string

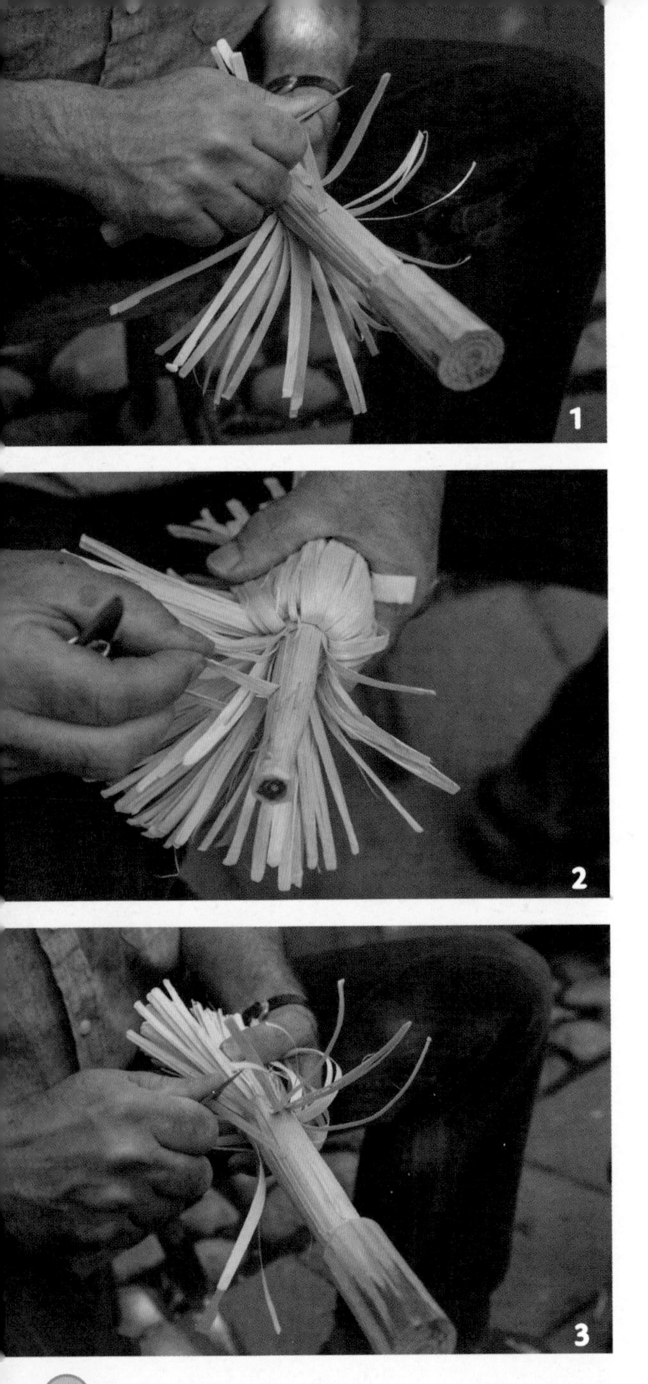

How to make it

1. Strip the bark of half the branch, then start pulling up fibres by making a small notch at a 45° angle and pulling the wood fibres towards your body (see wood carving technique 6 on p. 20).
2. As seen in Figure 1, carefully pull up a strip with a knife and your thumb, if necessary use a leather thumb guard. The first fibres will be short so pull them right off. Continue pulling fibres up around the branch until they are 10–12 cm (4–5 in) long. Use your hand holding the workpiece as a stopper so you don't pull them right off by mistake.
3. Once you have pulled the fibres up a little, you can use your fingers to continue pulling (see Figure 2). Turn the branch around and remove the rest of the bark.
4. Pull up the fibres in the same way, leaving a gap of around 1 cm (½ in). Start far enough up the branch so the fibres are around 2 cm (1 in) longer (see Figure 3). Don't pull up as many fibres on this end as the branch is also the handle.

5. Carve the handle, and if you want to, top it with a sphere for decoration.
6. Cut or whittle away the wood remaining in the centre and fold down the top fibres over the bottom fibres (see Figure 4).
7. Tie all the fibres together with a willow twig, a leather thong or string (see Figure 5).

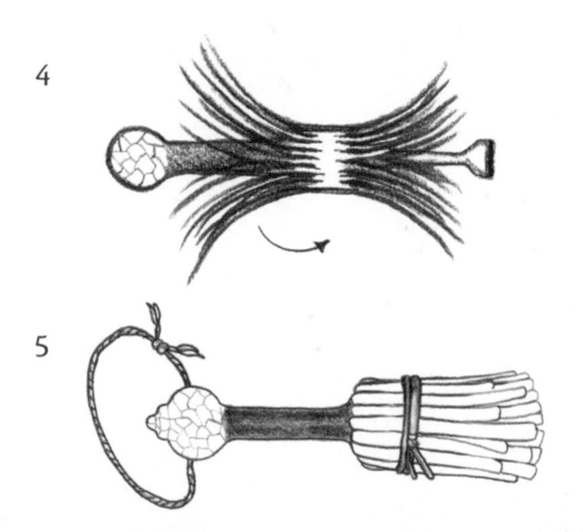

KITCHEN ROLL HOLDER*

This is a fun project to make and a great gift idea. Test your whittling skills by making a more complex decoration for the top.

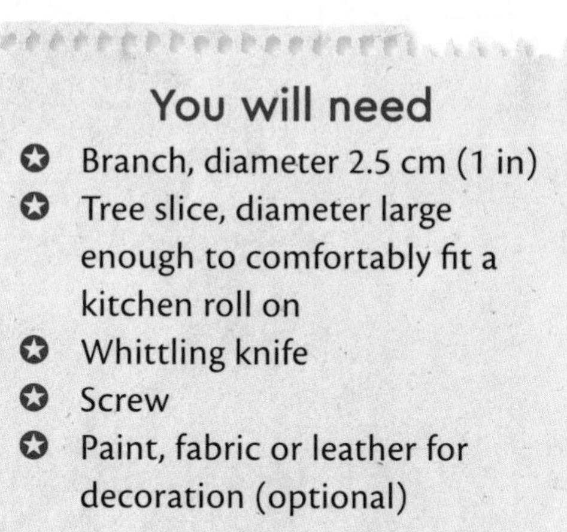

You will need

- Branch, diameter 2.5 cm (1 in)
- Tree slice, diameter large enough to comfortably fit a kitchen roll on
- Whittling knife
- Screw
- Paint, fabric or leather for decoration (optional)

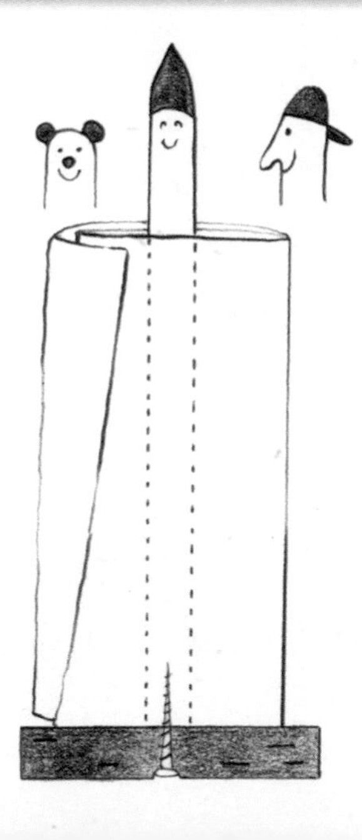

How to make it

1. Carve a figure or any other decoration you like on one end of the branch, for example a simple gnome, a man with a hat and leather or fabric brim, a carefully worked sphere, or a small bear with a muzzle and fabric ears. The choice is completely up to you.
2. Connect the branch and tree slice with a screw. You will need to countersink the screw so it won't scratch any surfaces when the holder is placed upright (see figure).
3. Paint or decorate your holder if you want to.

HOLLOWING OUT A BRANCH**

You will need

- Branch without side branches or knots, diameter suited to its later use; the workpiece needs to be slightly longer than the finished project so you can clamp it securely while you drill a hole
- Whittling knife
- Saw
- Drill, hand drill, or centre bit, diameter 15–30 mm ($^{19}/_{32}$–$1^{3}/_{16}$ in)
- Protective glove
- If you want to make a shrunken box, which requires a longer length of branch, you will need a long sharp knife

You can easily hollow out a branch and use it for all sorts of things, for example a decorative egg cup (see opposite), or a shrunken box (see p. 132).

How to make it

1. Clamp the branch to a table and drill a hole in the centre as deep as you need it to be.
2. Saw off the drilled length.
3. Wear a glove and "peel" away the wood inside with your knife, either turning the wood or the knife until the hole is the right size.
4. Push the knife far enough into the hole so it does not slip; the tip can stick out the other side.
5. You can carve decorative patterns into the bark, depending on your branch's intended use.

EGG CUP**

A hollowed out branch is perfect for an egg cup and you won't need to make a base. You can create a simple egg cup holder for several egg cups (see photo on the right) by making a miniature kitchen roll holder (see p. 117).

You will need

- Branch, diameter 5 cm (2 in), length 15–20 cm (6–8 in)
- Drill, diameter 20–25 mm ($^{25}/_{32}$–$^{63}/_{64}$ in)
- Whittling knife
- Saw
- Protective glove
- Paint or linseed oil for decoration

How to make it

1. Drill a hole through the centre and cut a length of branch 3–4 cm (1¼–1½ in) wide. Whittle the hole circular to fit an egg.
2. See instructions opposite for how to hollow out a branch with a knife.
3. Decorate the egg cup with patterns, strip the bark and sand it smooth, or leave the whittled knife strokes.
4. Leave to dry and then paint or oil.

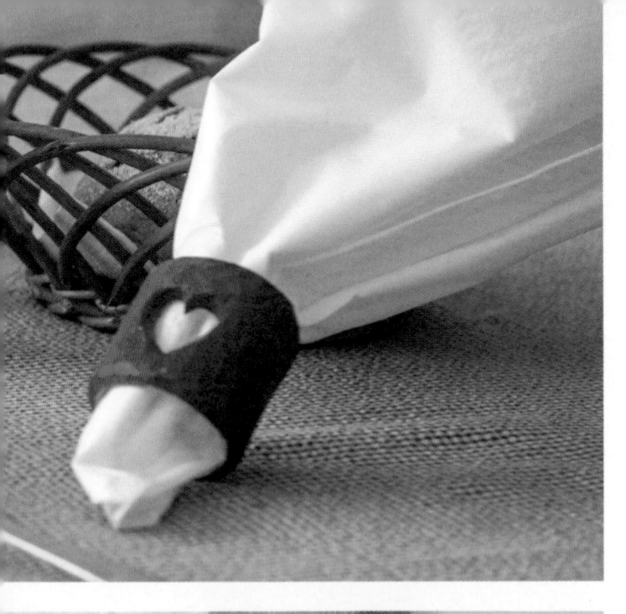

RINGS**

How to make it

Napkin ring and scout's neckerchief slide:

1. Make the napkin ring and the neckerchief slide in the same way as the egg cup (see p.119), but with a smaller diameter.
2. To create the heart in the napkin ring, drill two holes and then carefully carve the heart shape.

Finger ring:

1. You can make a finger ring out of a small piece of elder branch by pushing the pith out and then whittling the ring into a circular shape. It is a good idea to use a thimble or a glove for this. When the ring is dry it will shrink into a slight oval, so leave enough wood to whittle it round again.
2. Be careful – the ring will shrink significantly during the drying process, so only wear it on your finger once it is completely dry!

REFRIGERATOR MAGNETS**

Why not make your own fridge magnets? It can be lots of fun creating different characters!

You will need

- Branch, diameter 4 cm (1½ in), length 7–10 cm (2¾–4 in), if you want a nose or beak you will need a piece of wood with a side branch
- Magnets; there are different kinds, e.g. solid magnetic discs, magnet sheets which can be cut to size or self-adhesive magnetic tape; some are stronger than others
- Whittling knife
- Wood glue
- Paint for decoration (optional)

How to make it

1. Saw or split the branch lengthways. Side branches can give the figures an interesting profile or stick out as a nose or beak.
2. Carve the figure, but make the back completely flat.
3. Once the wood has dried, glue the magnet to the back and decorate your figure.

SMALL SIGNS*

These signs have many uses: attach them to doors and drawers, or use them as gift tags or key rings.

You will need

- Branch, diameter 2–4 cm (1–1½ in), long enough to hold while whittling
- Whittling knife
- Ink or paint for decoration (optional)

How to make it

1. As shown in the figure below, split the branch and then split one half again.
2. Whittle both sides of the twice-split branch flat, round or with decorative grooves if you would like to.
3. Leave your piece to dry and then decorate it, depending on what you're going to use your sign for.

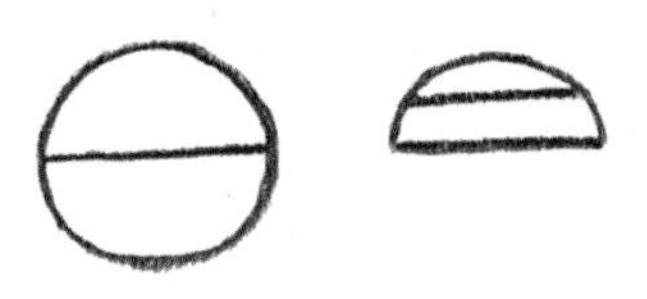

PENCILS*

You will need

- Branch, the same length as the pencil lead, diameter 1–1.5 cm (½–¾ in)
- Pencil lead, diameter at least 2 mm, but better 3–5 mm (approx. ¼ in) as it is less likely to break. You can buy lead and coloured pencil leads in most craft and art stores.
- Drill, same diameter as pencil lead
- Whittling knife
- Paint for decoration (optional)

How to make it

1. Clamp the branch to a table or bench and drill a hole for the pencil as far as the drill reaches. If necessary, make the hole slightly larger by moving the drill back and forth while drilling.
2. Carefully push the pencil lead into the hole. If you use fresh branches the pencil lead will sit tight once the branch has dried and shrunk.
3. Carve figures or patterns while the branch is still fresh.
4. Once the pencil lead fits securely, whittle the tip. Work carefully so you don't whittle away too much of the pencil lead.
5. Paint or decorate however you like.

KNOBS AND COAT HOOKS*

Knobs for drawers or cupboards and coat hooks are simple to make, but can be fun and satisfying projects for wood carving beginners.

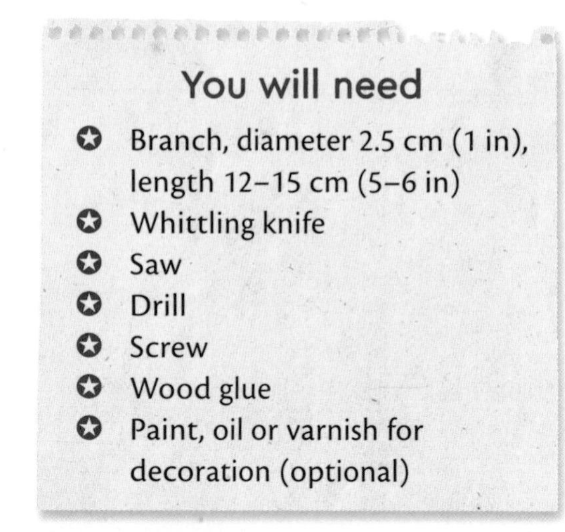

You will need

- Branch, diameter 2.5 cm (1 in), length 12–15 cm (5–6 in)
- Whittling knife
- Saw
- Drill
- Screw
- Wood glue
- Paint, oil or varnish for decoration (optional)

How to make it

1. Whittle the knob or hook shape towards the centre of the branch following the direction of the arrows in Figure 1. By using this method, you won't need to whittle towards yourself and you can make two knobs or hooks out of each branch.
2. Separate the knobs or hooks with a saw or knife and round the ends a bit more.
3. Saw the knob or hook to the length you need.

4. There are several ways to attach a knob or hook (see Figure 2):
    - Insert a long screw through a hole drilled right through the knob/hook (see Figure 2a).
    - Screw from the back into the knob/hook (Figure 2b).
    - Drill a hole in the back of the knob/hook, saw the screw head off and glue into the knob/hook (Figure 2c).

1

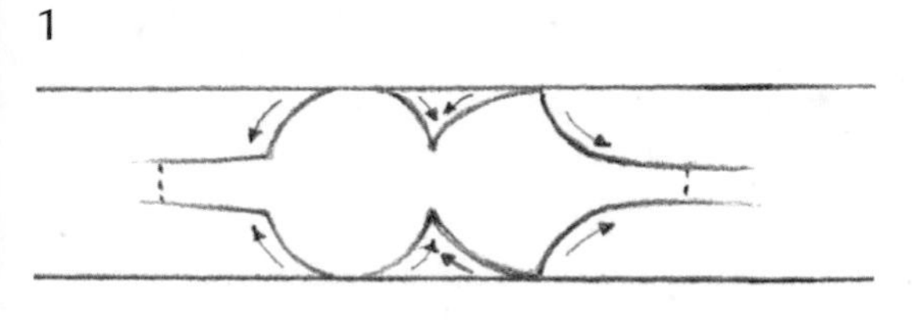

2

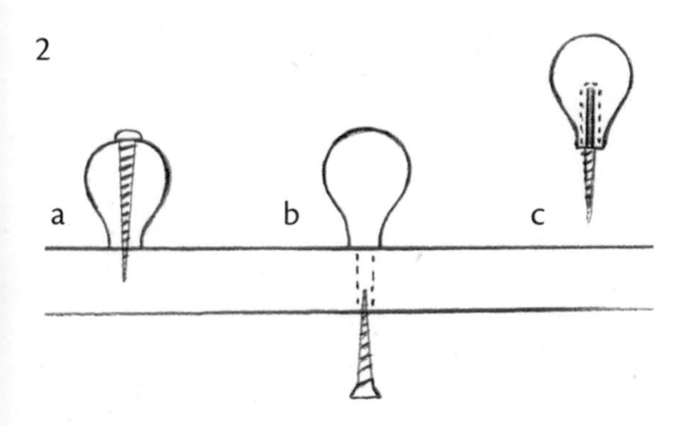

WALL HOOKS*

You can make a simple hook board, or more experienced whittlers may want to try some decorative shapes. The hooks can either be simple dowels, twigs, or you can carve them yourself.

You will need

- Branch, diameter 4–5 cm (1½–2 in)
- Dowel or dry twigs, diameter 5–10 mm (¼–½)
- Drill
- Screws
- Whittling knife
- Saw
- Wood glue
- Paint for decoration (optional)

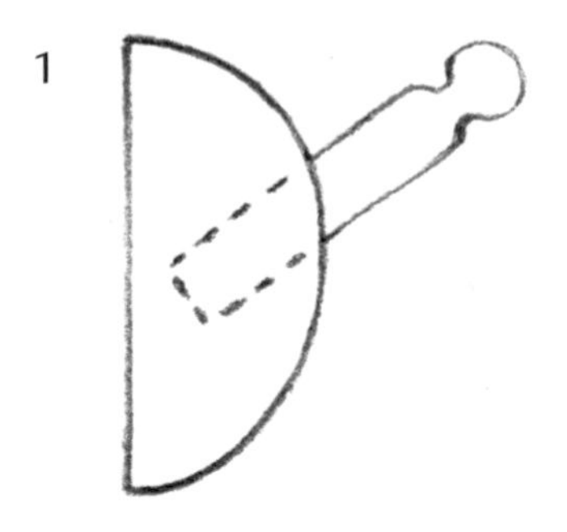

How to make it

1. Split or saw the branch in half lengthways.
2. If necessary, whittle the back straight. Shape your branch as you please (see photos for ideas).
3. To make the hooks, round the twigs or dowels on one end and saw or cut to the length you want; remember some of the length will disappear in the hole. Make as many hooks as you need.
4. Drill the holes for the hooks at an angle (see Figure 1) and glue the hooks in place.
5. Drill small holes at each end of the board to screw to the wall.

HANGING HOOKS**

Discarded Christmas trees are great for whittling. You can make decorative hanging hooks, or even a bird's nest for your garden.

You will need

- Branch where most of the length is above the side branches. The second ring of branches is usually the correct size.
- Whittling knife
- Drill
- String
- Paint, oil or varnish (optional)

How to make it

1. Strip the bark. Work carefully and exactly, particularly the tricky bits between the main branch and side branches. It's likely you'll get resin on your hands so it's best to wear gloves.
2. Round the ends and sand them if you want a smooth finish. You can whittle figures or designs in the main branch to decorate the hooks.
3. Drill a hole in the top part of the trunk (see figure) and knot the string in place.
4. If you want to, paint or varnish your hanging hooks.

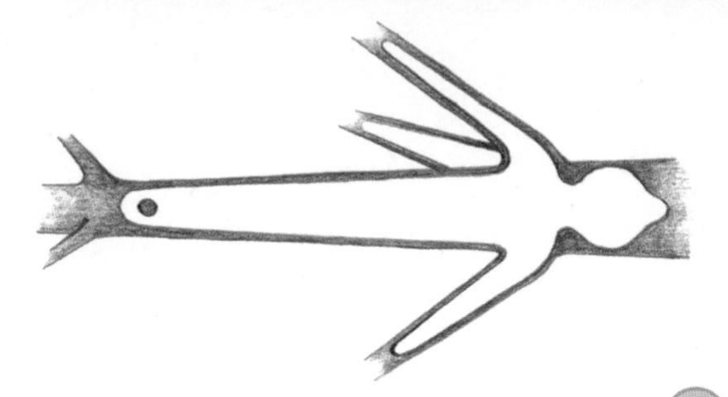

CANDLESTICK*

You will need

- Branch, diameter 4–5 cm (1½–2 in)
- Whittling knife
- Metal candle cup, 12–14 mm (approx. ½–¾ in)
- Small screw
- Candle, diameter to fit the candle cup
- Paint for decoration (optional)

Tip:

Pillar candleholder

The height of the candlestick is dependent on the size and weight of the branch; if necessary, attach a larger tree slice as a base to stabilise it.

Vertical candleholder

The branch should be split or sawn in half lengthways.

Making a pillar or flat candleholder is a fairly simple project. The candlestick on the photo opposite is a little more advanced (***) and is made out of the tip of a Christmas tree with small birds perched on the side branches. To make this kind of candlestick, follow the hanging hook instructions on p. 127 and find out how to make the birds on p. 33.

How to make it

1. Whittle the shape of the candleholder. You can make decorative patterns or even create a figure.
2. Screw the cup in place or drill a hole to insert it into. Make sure to countersink the screw from below so your candle sits flat on a surface.
3. If you want to, paint or decorate your candlestick.

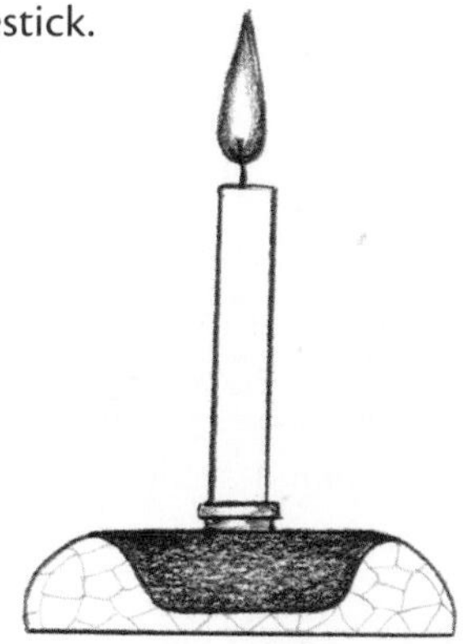

KEY RINGS*

You will need

- Small branch, thick enough not to break when whittled
- Drill, diameter 5 mm ($^{13}/_{64}$ in)
- Whittling knife
- Metal key ring, diameter 3 cm (1¼ in)
- Paint or oil for decoration

Use your imagination and create some fun and individual key rings.

How to make it

1. Whittle the branch into the desired shape and narrow one end for the key ring. Use the same carving technique as when making knobs/hooks and whittle from the centre of the branch (see p. 124).
2. Drill a hole and attach the key ring.
3. Paint or apply oil. Have fun creating characters, and use bright colours to make sure you never lose your keys again!

CROCODILE CLOTHES PEG**

Carving a crocodile peg can be quite tricky as it's such a fine and small project, but it's lots of fun once you get it right. You can even add a magnet to the back of your crocodile to create a characterful fridge magnet too.

You will need

- Wooden clothes peg
- Whittling knife
- Paint or ink for decoration (optional)

How to make it

1. Pull the peg apart so you have two separate halves.
2. Whittle the crocodile's head slightly narrower and carve tiny grooves for teeth. Create eyes and nostrils on the upper part of the peg (as seen in photo).
3. Whittle a pointed tail, and if you want to, create a small side curve on the body as well.
4. Make small grooves in the crocodile's back.
5. If you'd like to, decorate your crocodile peg with paint or ink.

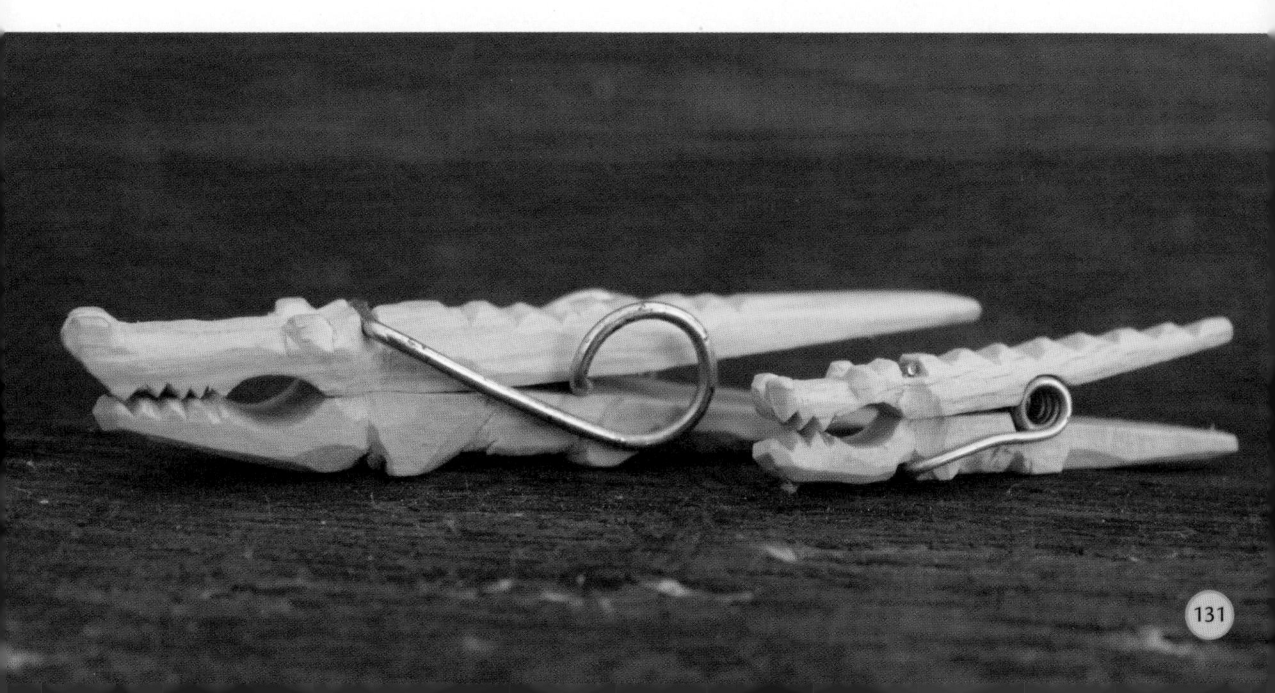

SHRUNKEN BOX***

You will need

- Branch, diameter 5–8 cm (2–3¼ in), length 6–8 cm (2½– 3¼ in)
- Dry wood for the base (lime wood or basswood is best), 4–8 mm (approx. ¼–½ in) thick
- Drill, 18–24 mm (23⁄32–15⁄16 in)
- Knife (a thinner and slightly longer blade than usual), 7–12 cm (2¾–5 in)
- Homemade marking gauge (optional, see instructions on p. 135)

The secret of a shrunken box is that the wood contracts or shrinks as it dries. Use this to your advantage and make a box where the base attaches itself seemingly by magic!

Make the shrunken box out of a branch with or without bark, and design the shape and decorations as you please. If you want to, you can make a lid for your box too.

How to make it

1. Drill a hole in the branch and hollow out so the wood is around 1 cm (½ in) thick (see "Hollowing out a branch", p. 118 for instructions). It is important that the wood does not dry and shrink before the base is put in place, so if necessary, keep the wood in a plastic bag in the fridge.
2. Carve a 2–3 mm deep groove right around the inside of the box (see Figure 2); this can be difficult so work carefully. To do this, make two grooves on the inside of the branch, the first 1 cm (½ in) away from the edge, the second 2–3 mm further away from that. There are two ways to do this:
   - Sketch two lines in the correct place and whittle along them with the tip of your knife. Remove the wood between the grooves.
   - Using the marking gauge (see instructions for making on p. 135), scratch the two grooves (Figure 1).

   Hold the marking gauge and turn the wood. Remove the remaining wood with the tip of the knife or the tip of the marking gauge.
3. Place the base under the box and draw the outline with a sharp lead pencil (see Figure 3). Mark the exact position of the base by drawing lines on the base piece and the inside of the box. Saw or whittle out the base, and remember to check whether it fits. It should only just fit in the box piece.
4. Whittle the edges of the base; the edge should be slightly narrower than the groove inside the box.
5. Place the base in the groove and wait! Will the box shrink enough to hold the base in place? Or will it shrink too much and split? Keep the shrunken box in a cool place and be patient – it can take several days for wood to dry completely, so keep checking.
6. Once it's completely dry, you can carve patterns into your box, or paint it to decorate.

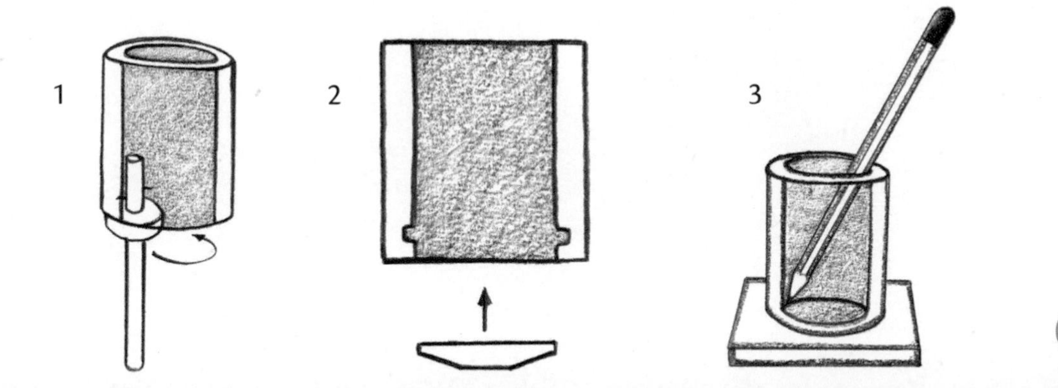

Lid:

1. Once the box is completely dry, you can make a lid out of dry wood by placing a piece of paper over the top of the box and scratching along the inside with a nail or marking with a pencil.
2. Cut out the lid template.
3. To make a simple lid, glue the cut out lid to a larger piece of wood (see Figure 4).
4. To make a more difficult version, whittle the lid out of a single piece of wood instead (see Figure 5).

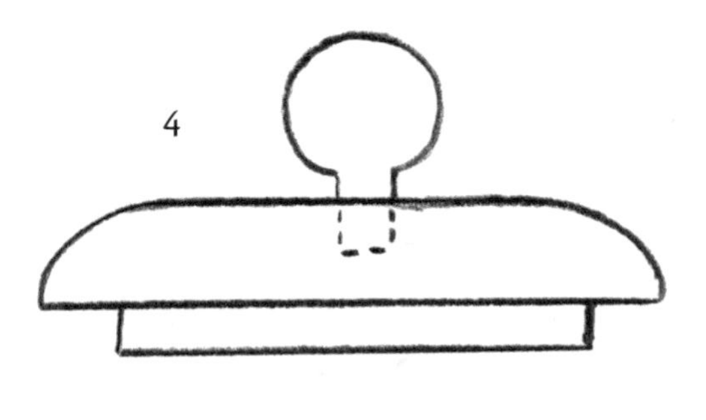

MARKING GAUGE*

As demonstrated in the previous project, a marking gauge is a useful tool to have. However, if you don't want to make your own, they are widely available in most hardware and DIY stores.

You will need

- Dowel, diameter 10 mm (½ in), length 12–15 cm (5–6 in)
- Wood piece/wood ring with a 10 mm (½ in) hole
- Two nails, diameter 1.5–2 mm (¾–1⁄16 in)
- Drill, same diameter as the nails (1⁄16–5⁄64 in)
- Wood glue
- Metal file

How to make it

1. Glue the wood ring to the dowel, 2–3 cm (1–1¼ in) away from one end.
2. File the tip of each nail to a sharp, miniature blade.
3. Drill two holes for the nails in the dowel, one around 1 cm (½ in) below the wood ring, the other on the opposite side of the dowel, around 2–3 mm further up (see photo below).
4. Cut the tips off the nails and then hammer or glue them into the holes. The tips should stick out about 3 mm (just under ¼ in), with the sharpened blade pointing in the cutting direction.